30-DAY JAPANESE LEARNING QUEST *for* BEGINNERS

From Zero to Confident:
Master Essential Conversation,
Travel & Anime Phrases
(Just 10 Mins a Day)

Naomi Sato

Contents

★ EXCLUSIVE FREE READER BONUSES ★

Congratulations on your commitment to learning Japanese!

I've created special bonuses just for you. These bonuses are my way of supporting your Japanese learning journey. I hope they help!

Arigatou gozaimasu!

- ✔ Secret Bonus Quest to push you beyond beginner level.
- ✔ Quest Master Certificate: Your achievement badge to celebrate success.
- ✔ Flashcards

SCAN THE QR CODE TO DOWNLOAD COMPLEMENTARY BONUSES FOR YOUR QUEST

Introduction

The first time I tried to learn Japanese, I gave up.

Not because I didn't care. Not because I didn't try. But because everything I tried felt··· wrong. Too academic. Too complicated. Too disconnected from how people actually talk.

I remember sitting at my desk, flipping flashcards like a blackjack dealer—hiragana, katakana, kanji. Everything blurred together into symbols I couldn't see my way through. I'd listen to a Japanese podcast, thinking, *Did they just say five words, or was that one really long one?*

I'd bought the books. I downloaded the apps. I even tried one of those "Learn Japanese While You Sleep" audios (spoiler alert: I woke up still confused).

Eventually, I realized I wasn't failing at learning Japanese; I was failing at using someone else's method. One that wasn't built for how real people speak, live, or connect.

So I started from scratch.

I gave myself permission to learn just 10 minutes a day. I focused on real-world phrases—the ones you actually use when meeting someone, asking for help, or grabbing dinner. And I made it fun. Relatable. Human.

A year later, I was traveling through Japan, ordering food, navigating stations, and having conversations with locals who didn't know that Japanese was my second language. I wasn't "fluent." But I was comfortable. Capable. Conversational.

And that changed everything.

What This Book Is

This book is the resource I wish I had from the beginning: a mission-based guide that treats you like a curious, capable human, not a student preparing for an exam.

Every day, you'll complete a short "quest"—a quick, friendly mission that helps you speak, understand, or connect. A goal with purpose. You'll learn how to:

- Greet someone with confidence.
- Ask for directions or recommendations.
- Order food at a ramen shop.
- Understand key words in anime.
- Pick up context clues in conversation.
- Read and write kana.
- Recognize essential kanji.
- Use cultural gestures to build real connections.

By the end of each week, you'll earn a Gem—a symbol of your progress and growth.

There are 5 weekly quests, each focused on a real-world theme (like meeting people, ordering food, or watching anime). Complete them, and you'll collect all 5 Gems, ready for the final boss: Week 6.

Each Gem quest is designed to help you feel progress, not pressure.

And you'll do it in minutes a day, with phrases you can actually use, not ones you'll forget after the quiz.

Who This Book Is For

This book is for you if:

- You've always wanted to learn Japanese but didn't know where to start.
- You've tried before, got overwhelmed, and gave up.
- You love Japanese culture, anime, food, or travel, and want to connect on a deeper level.
- You're busy, but you've got 10 minutes a day.

You don't need to be a genius. You don't need a photographic memory. You just need curiosity, consistency, and this book in your hands.

By the end, you'll be able to:

- Hold basic conversations with native speakers.
- Recognize key kanji that show up all over Japan.
- Understand and use foundational grammar patterns.
- Handle daily life in Japan: shopping, dining, directions.
- Catch words in your favorite anime and music.

And most importantly, feel confident using Japanese.

- You'll also be introduced to Japanese grammar particles like:
  - » は (*wa*) – the topic marker
  - » を (*o*) – the object marker
  - » に (*ni*) and で (*de*) – time/place indicators

These little words may seem confusing at first, but you'll get to know them naturally through examples, conversations, and context.

Each one will be explained as it appears, so there's no memorizing without meaning.

How This Book Works

You'll go on a 6-week journey, with each week focused on a theme (like greetings, travel, or pop culture), and each day giving you a mini mission.

Every daily lesson includes:

- A practical mission (order food, ask directions, make a friend)
- 3–4 real-life phrases
- One beginner-friendly kanji
- A short dialogue
- A cultural or anime insight
- A journal to write your favorite things from each week (you can find it at the end of this book)

And more!

Every lesson is designed to take about 10 minutes. No cramming. No cringing. Just steady, joyful growth.

Why I Wrote This Book

I didn't write this as a language expert. I wrote it as someone who struggled, who almost gave up, and who finally found a way that worked.

I've always loved Japanese, the way it sounds, the rhythm of its respect, the culture that flows through every syllable. But learning it the traditional way left me feeling like an outsider. This book is about making you feel like you belong.

Whether you want to travel, connect with Japanese friends, understand your favorite shows without subtitles, or just prove to yourself that you can, you're in the right place.

Let's flip the script together.

You don't need to be fluent to connect. You don't need to be perfect to begin. You just need 10 minutes. Every day.

Ready? 行こう! (*Ikou!* Let's go!)

Week 1: Foundations of Japanese Interaction

Welcome to Week 1—your first official step into the world of Japanese.

Not the textbook version. Not the overwhelming, grammar-packed, academic maze version. The real version. The version that helps you walk into a shop and say "hello." Order your first drink. Say "thank you," and mean it. Hear something in an anime and think, *Wait—I understood that!*

This week is about learning what actually matters when you're first starting out: how to greet someone, how to be polite, how to ask for something simple, and how to count to five without breaking a sweat.

That's it.

These may sound small, but they're huge. Because the moment you confidently say "こんにちは" (*kon-ni-chi-wa*) and see someone smile in return? That's the spark. That's when the language stops being a wall and starts becoming a bridge.

What You'll Learn This Week

This week, you'll learn:

- How to say hello, thank you, excuse me, and nice to meet you.
- How to make simple requests like "this, please."
- How to count from 1 to 5.
- How to ask "how much?" when shopping.
- Your first five essential kanji (person, one, two, yen).
- How to recognize politeness in everyday Japanese.
- How bowing works—and where it shows up in anime.

Why These First Phrases Matter

The most powerful thing you can do in a new language isn't perfect grammar. It's kindness. Politeness. Presence. And that's what Japanese thrives on.

You'll hear these phrases everywhere. They're the base of conversations in restaurants, trains, shops, schools—even anime battles. If you've ever heard someone yell "すみません!" (*su-mi-ma-sen!*) while charging into action··· yeah, that's the one.

You'll also start recognizing kanji, those mysterious characters that once looked like ancient symbols but will soon start making total sense. This week introduces some of the easiest, most common ones—no stress, just progress.

How Japanese Sounds Work

Oh, and before we continue, I want you to keep in mind this very important detail: Japanese is refreshingly consistent. No silent letters, no tricky spellings. Just a few basics to keep in mind:

- **Vowels stay the same:** A = "ah;" E = "eh;" I = "ee;" O = "oh;" U = "oo." (Example: ありがとう = a-ri-ga-to-u)
- **R sounds soft** – halfway between **R, L,** and **D.** Try: らりるれろ = ra-ri-ru-re-ro
- **No L sounds** in native Japanese—just that soft R.

Speak slowly, repeat out loud, and trust your tongue to catch up.

You don't need to be fluent yet. You just need to keep showing up.

So grab your pen, flex your vocal cords, and let's start where it all begins—with a simple, powerful "Hello."

Day 1: Greet Like a Local

01

Mission: Start a Conversation With Confidence

Let's get something out of the way: You do not need to master 2,000 kanji or memorize textbook dialogues to start speaking Japanese.

What you do need is the courage to say one word: こんにちは。(*kon-ni-chi-wa.*)

That one word opens doors.

This is where it starts. Day 1. You're about to learn how to greet someone with confidence, show basic politeness, and introduce yourself like a kind, respectful human being, which, if we're being honest, is what language learning is all about.

You're not here to pass a test. You're here to connect.

So let's make that connection. And let's make it simple.

Phrases of the Day

Japanese	Pronunciation	Meaning
こんにちは	*kon-ni-chi-wa*	Hello / Good afternoon
ありがとう	*a-ri-ga-tou*	Thank you
すみません	*su-mi-ma-sen*	Excuse me / I'm sorry
はじめまして	*ha-ji-me-ma-shi-te*	Nice to meet you

Quick Breakdown

- **こんにちは *(kon-ni-chi-wa)***: Used from late morning to early evening. Friendly, respectful, and easy to remember.

Think of it as the Japanese "Hey there!" but with a little more polish.

- ありがとう ***(a-ri-ga-tou)***: A casual thank you. Pair it with a smile, and it's perfect for daily use.
- すみません ***(su-mi-ma-sen)***: Hugely versatile. Use it to say excuse me, get someone's attention, or offer a light apology. You'll say this a lot—especially in train stations!
- はじめまして ***(ha-ji-me-ma-shi-te)***: Said the first time you meet someone. It means "Nice to meet you," but also carries the meaning of "This is our beginning."

Pro Tip: Say each phrase out loud right now. Don't worry about sounding perfect. You're warming up your ears and your mouth.

Kanji, Kana, and Why Japanese Has So Many "Looks"

Before we continue, I'd like to introduce you to kanji and kana. In this book, you'll learn a symbol every day.

At first, Japanese writing can look like a chaotic mix of symbols, I know. That's because the language uses three writing systems—but don't worry, they each have a role, and you'll learn to tell them apart naturally.

Hiragana (ひらがな)

- Curvy, simple characters
- Used for native Japanese words, grammar endings, and beginners' books
- Example: たべます (*ta-be-ma-su* = to eat)

Katakana (カタカナ)

- Sharp, angular characters

- Used for foreign words, sound effects, names, and emphasis
- Example: パン (*pan* = bread, borrowed from French)

Kanji (漢字)

- Complex, Chinese-origin characters
- Used for most nouns, verbs, adjectives, and concepts
- Each one carries meaning, not just sound
- Example: 食 (*eat*), 学 (*study*), 水 (*water*)

So, Why Do They Look Different From What You Say?

Let's take the word "eat."

- Spoken = たべます (*ta-be-masu*)
- Kanji = 食べます

You'll notice the verb stem 食 (read as "*ta*" in this case) is written with kanji, while the verb ending べます stays in hiragana. This is super common in Japanese—most sentences are a blend of kanji and hiragana.

Think of kanji as "meaning blocks," and hiragana as "grammar glue."

And don't worry, I'll only introduce kanji slowly, starting with the ones you'll see everywhere in Japan.

At the end of this book, you'll have access to 40+ foundational kanji without memorizing long lists—just by seeing them in real phrases and everyday situations.

Ready? Your first kanji is up next.

Kanji of the Day: 人

- **Meaning:** Person
- **Reading:** ひと (*hi-to*)

- **Mnemonic:** Looks like someone walking on two legs—just like you starting your language journey.

This is one of the most fundamental kanji. You'll see it in:

- 人々 (*hi-to-bi-to*) – people
- 日本人 (*ni-hon-jin*) – Japanese person
- 一人 (*hi-to-ri*) – one person

The symbol is simple, elegant, and everywhere.

Stroke Order

You might be wondering if kanji has a stroke order. The answer is yes, let's learn about it:

What Is Stroke Order?

Stroke order is the correct sequence of lines that form a kanji. Following it helps you:

- Remember kanji more easily.
- Write neatly and naturally.
- Use Japanese apps and dictionaries more effectively.

Basic Stroke Rules

Think of stroke order like drawing a picture where there's a natural flow. Here are the golden rules:

- Top to bottom
- Left to right
- Horizontal before vertical
- Outside before inside
- Close the shape last

What Is a Radical?

A radical is a small part of a kanji that gives you a clue about its meaning. You'll see common ones pop up again and again—like 人 (person) or 水 (water).

Understood? Now, let's take a look at your first kanji's stroke order:

1. Left diagonal (top down)
2. Right diagonal (starts above and crosses slightly below the first)

Try It Yourself: Practice tracing it on your palm or a notebook three times. Each time you write it, say the word out loud: *hito... hito... hito.*

That's it! You don't need to memorize rules—just keep an eye on the patterns and practice tracing each kanji a few times as you learn it.

Mini-Dialogue: Polite First Meeting

Here's your first real-life mini-scene:

A. こんにちは！(*ko-n-ni-chi-wa*) [Hello!]

B. はじめまして。(*ha-ji-me-ma-shi-te*) [Nice to meet you.]

A. ありがとう！(*a-ri-ga-tou*) [Thank you!]

B: すみません… (*su-mi-ma-sen*) [Excuse me…]

Simple? Yes. But this is the exact type of interaction you'll have over and over again—at meetups, language exchanges, travel tours, and anime conventions.

Even one of these words, spoken with sincerity, can create connection.

Cultural Insight: The Art of Bowing

In Japan, bowing isn't just a formality; it's a language all on its own.

A slight bow (about 15°) is the standard for greetings and casual thank-yous. You'll see this in schools, stores, train stations, and even in anime.

The bow says: *I see you. I respect you.* No words needed.

- **Anime Moment:** In *My Teen Romantic Comedy SNAFU*, even awkward teenagers bow when introducing themselves. It's that deeply ingrained in daily life.
- **Travel Tip:** When entering a store or receiving help from someone, pair your "ありがとう" (*a-ri-ga-tou*) or "すみません" (*su-mi-ma-sen*) with a gentle nod or bow. Even a subtle gesture makes a huge difference.

Quick Quiz – 1 Minute

Match the phrase to its meaning:

1. はじめまして	a. Excuse me / I'm sorry
2. すみません	b. Hello
3. こんにちは	c. Nice to meet you
4. ありがとう	d. Thank you

Bonus Practice: Try saying one of these phrases out loud to yourself or a friend today. Even better, record yourself saying all four!

Answers: 1–c, 2–a, 3–b, 4–d

XP Earned: 20

You've completed your first mission!

Badge Progress: Phrase Pioneer – 1/5 Days Complete (You'll unlock your badge at the end of Day 5.)

Final Thoughts

You did it. You spoke your first Japanese. That's no small thing.

You've now got four essential expressions, a powerful kanji, and the cultural context to start using them with confidence. If all you did this week was repeat "こんにちは" (*kon-ni-chi-wa*) while walking around your apartment, you'd still be further than 90% of people who never start.

You're not just learning Japanese; you're living it.

And now, you're ready for Day 2, where you'll learn how to ask for *something politely*, like a bowl of ramen, a menu, or even… a favor.

Scan to Listen

3%.....Complete!!

Day 2: Polite Requests

02

Mission: Ask With Confidence—and Kindness

Here's something most language textbooks forget to tell you: Being polite in Japanese doesn't make you sound stiff; it makes you sound cool.

Seriously. In Japan, polite language is soft, intentional, and warm. It shows care. And when you use it, even just a little, you earn trust fast.

Today, you'll learn how to ask for something, how to say "please," and how to respond when someone hands you something. These are phrases you'll use constantly, whether you're in a restaurant, shopping, or just being your thoughtful self.

They're short. They're simple. And they're magic.

Phrases of the Day

Japanese	Pronunciation	Meaning
おねがいします	*o-ne-gai-shi-ma-su*	Please (formal/humble request)
ください	*ku-da-sai*	Please give me...
どうぞ	*dou-zo*	Here you go / Go ahead
はじめま ありがとうございます して	*a-ri-ga-tou go-zai-ma-su*	Thank you very much (formal)

How to Use Them

- おねがいします ***(o-ne-gai-shi-ma-su)***: This is your go-to phrase when you're asking for a service, ordering politely, or wrapping up a request. You can say it alone or after what you want. For example: "メニュー、おねがいします。" (*me-nyu, o-ne-gai shi-ma-su*).
- ください ***(ku-da-sai)***: Use this when you want something specific, especially a physical item. Point to a dish on a menu or a bottle in a store and say "これ、ください" (*ko-re, ku-da-sai*).
- どうぞ ***(dou-zo)***: This is what you say when offering something: a seat, a gift, directions. It shows you're being considerate.
- ありがとうございます ***(a-ri-ga-tou go-zai-ma-su)***: A step up from "ありがとう" (*a-ri-ga-tou*), this version is more formal, respectful, and professional. Say it to shopkeepers, waitstaff, strangers, or anyone who's done something kind for you.

Say them out loud:

- *O-ne-ga-i-shi-ma-su...*
- *Ku-da-sa-i...*
- *Dou-zo...*
- *A-ri-ga-tou go-za-i-ma-su...*

Now try whispering them, then saying them confidently with a smile.

Kanji of the Day: 手

- **Meaning:** Hand
- **Reading:** て (*te*)

- Mnemonic: Imagine an open hand with five fingers. It's giving, reaching, or receiving—just like your polite phrases today.

You'll see this kanji in words like:

- 手紙 (*te-ga-mi*) – letter
- 上手 (*jou-zu*) – skilled (literally, "upper hand")
- 握手 (*a-ku-shu*) – handshake

Stroke Order

1. A horizontal top line
2. A short vertical stroke in the center
3. A long curved stroke (like a wrist)
4. Two short strokes underneath (like fingers)

Try it out: Write it three times on paper or in the air. Say *te... te... te* with each stroke. That's how muscle memory starts.

Mini-Dialogue: Making a Polite Request

A: コーヒー、おねがいします。(*Koo-hii, o-ne-gai-shi-masu.*)

B: はい、どうぞ。(*Hai, dou-zo.*)

A: ありがとうございます！(*A-ri-ga-tou go-zai-ma-su!*)

Try swapping "coffee" for:

- メニュー (*men-yuu*) – menu
- みず (*mi-zu*) – water
- チケット (*chi-ke-tto*) – ticket

Cultural Insight: The Beauty of Politeness

Japanese is a way of interacting with the world. And politeness is one of its most beautiful features.

From childhood, people in Japan are taught to soften their requests. Not to demand. Not to push. But to ask with grace. You'll hear "おねがいします" (*O-ne-gai shi-ma-su*) dozens of times a day—at restaurants, on the train, even during anime battle scenes.

- **Anime Moment:** In *Demon Slayer*, Tanjiro, even while facing demons, never forgets his manners. He says "おねがいします" (*o-ne-gai-shi-ma-su*) when asking for guidance and "ありがとうございます" (*a-ri-ga-tou go-zai-ma-su*) even in the toughest moments. It's not weakness; it's strength with humility.
- **Travel Tip:** When in doubt, say "おねがいします" (*o-ne-gai-shi-ma-su*) or "ありがとうございます" (*a-ri-ga-tou go-zai-ma-su*) with a slight bow. Even if you mess up the grammar, people will notice—and appreciate—your effort.

Quick Quiz – 1 Minute

Choose the best response for each situation:

1. You want to order a drink. You say:
   a. すみません
   b. おねがいします
   c. ごめんなさい
2. Someone hands you a menu. You say:
   a. どうぞ
   b. おねがいします
   c. ありがとうございます

3. You hand someone a flyer. You say:

    a. どうぞ
    b. ください
    c. はじめまして

Bonus Task: Practice this 3-line dialogue out loud: "みず、ください。" – "はい、どうぞ。" – "ありがとうございます。" (*Mi-zu, ku-da-sai, Hai, dou-zo, A-ri-ga-tou go-zai-ma-su*).

Answers: 1–b, 2–c, 3–a

XP Earned: 20

Another mission complete!

Badge Progress: Phrase Pioneer – 2/5 Days Complete.

Final Thoughts

Asking for things is about tone. Timing. Trust.

In Japanese, small phrases carry big energy. "おねがいします" (*o-ne-gai-shi-ma-su*) can mean "please," but also: I respect you. I'm counting on you. I appreciate your help.

And guess what? You just learned how to say all that in under 10 minutes.

Take a breath. Let it sink in. You're learning more than just a language; you're learning how to move through another culture with presence.

Tomorrow, we start with something even more universal: numbers.

Let's count together, from ichi to go.

Scan to Listen

6%.....Complete!!

Day 3: Numbers 1–5

03

Mission: Count Clearly, Speak Confidently

Numbers are one of those things you don't think about until you really need them.

Like when you're ordering *gyoza* at a night market and the vendor asks how many you want, and you freeze, holding up fingers like a toddler while desperately whispering *"San? Go? Wait... Go is five, right?"*

I've been there.

That's why today's mission is all about mastering the first five numbers in Japanese: simple, powerful, and used everywhere. For paying something, asking for directions, or understanding an anime countdown before an epic transformation, these numbers are your foundation.

Let's make them second nature—without the stress.

Phrases of the Day

Japanese	Pronunciation	Meaning
いち	*Ichi*	1
に	*Ni*	2
さん	*San*	3
よん	*Yon*	4
ご	*Go*	5

Quick Tips

- You might hear し (*shi*) instead of よん for 4, and ご (*go*) is the same word used for "language" (e.g., *Ni-hon-go* = Japanese). Context will help you figure it out.
- For now, stick with よん—it's safer and more common, especially in counting.

Say it with me: Ichi, ni, san, yon, go. Try it three times, then whisper it backwards. Make it fun.

Kanji of the Day: 一 and 二

- 一 (***ichi***) – One. Mnemonic: One single line. Easy, right?
- 二 (***ni***) – Two. Mnemonic: Two parallel lines. No tricks here, what you see is what you get.

These are among the most beginner-friendly kanji in existence, and you just learned them both!

You'll soon spot them in:

- 一人 (*hi-to-ri*) – one person
- 二階 (*ni-kai*) – second floor
- 一番 (*i-chi-ban*) – number one / the best!

Stroke Order

一

1. One horizontal line (left to right)

二

1. Top horizontal line
2. Bottom horizontal line (slightly longer)

Try this: Write each kanji three times. Say the number as you write it. Your brain loves that connection between sound, motion, and meaning.

Mini-Dialogue: Counting in Action

A: いち、ください。(*I-chi, ku-da-sai.* – One, please.)

B: はい、さんぜんえんです。(*Hai, san-zen en desu.* – Okay, 3,000 yen.)

A: ありがとう！(*A-ri-ga-tou!* – Thanks!)

Now try this with other numbers:

- に、ください – Two, please
- ご、ください – Five, please

This is a real conversation you'll have with cashiers, shopkeepers, and food stalls. Short, polite, and perfectly functional.

Cultural Insight: Finger Counting, Japanese Style

Here's a surprise: the way you count on your fingers in Japan? It's different from how many Westerners do it.

In Japan, people start with an open palm and fold their fingers down to count. So:

- 1 = thumb down
- 2 = thumb + index finger down
- 3 = thumb + index + middle finger down, and so on
- **Anime Moment:** In *Naruto*, you'll often see ninjas using hand signs that involve counting or gestures; it's subtle, but it reflects Japan's visual culture and body language fluency.
- **Travel Tip:** Use your fingers and say the number aloud when ordering, especially in crowded markets or noisy train stations. Saying "さん" (*san*) while holding up three fingers is a winning combo.

Quick Quiz – 1 Minute

1. What does "よん" mean?
    a. 1
    b. 4
    c. 5
2. Which kanji represents "one"?
    a. 二
    b. 一
    c. 三
3. What would you say to order two items?
    a. に、ください
    b. さん、ください
    c. ご、ください

Challenge Mode: Try counting from 1–5 in Japanese with no peeking. Bonus points if you do it in front of a mirror.

Answers: 1–b, 2–b, 3–a

XP Earned: 20

You've now learned five powerful numbers and two more kanji. That's a big deal.

Badge Progress: Phrase Pioneer – 3/5 Days Complete

Final Thoughts

There's something empowering about learning to count in another language. It makes things feel real. Measurable. Yours.

Today, you moved from one to five. In another language. With a brand new writing system.

That's progress. Real, visible, speak-it-out-loud kind of progress.

So even if you're counting chopsticks at dinner or catching the word "さん" (*san*) in your favorite anime, take a second to feel proud. You're doing this.

And tomorrow? We're going shopping.

Let's learn how to ask, "How much is this?"—without looking like you're guessing.

Scan to Listen

10%.....Complete!!

Day 4: Shopping Basics

04

Mission: Buy Something Without the Panic

If you've ever been in a store abroad and just pointed at something while praying the cashier magically understood you··· you're not alone. I've done it: hands, smiles, awkward nods, maybe even interpretive dance.

But there's a better way.

Today's mission is all about one of the most essential travel skills: shopping. It can be at a convenience store in Tokyo, browsing a market in Osaka, or buying your first *gachapon* toy at an anime event. You need to know how to ask how much something costs and how to say "yes," "no," and "this, please" with confidence.

These are the phrases that turn you from a confused tourist into a curious explorer.

Let's make that moment smooth, polite, and (let's be honest) satisfying.

Phrases of the Day

Japanese	Pronunciation	Meaning
これはいくら?	*ko-re wa i-ku-ra?*	How much is this?
これ、ください	*ko-re, ku-da-sai*	This, please
はい	*ha-i*	Yes
いいえ	*ii-e*	No

How to Use Them

- これはいくら? ***(ko-re wa i-ku-ra?)***: Point to the item, hold it up if appropriate, and ask this. It literally means: "As for this, how much?" It's the perfect phrase for markets, shops, and food stalls.
- これ、ください ***(ko-re, ku-da-sai)***: Want it? Ask for it politely. This is how you say, "I'd like this one, please."
- はい ***(ha-i)*** and いいえ ***(ii-e)***: Two simple but powerful responses. "*Hai*" is "yes" (or "I understand"), while "*iie*" is "no" or a polite refusal. Use your tone and smile to keep things kind.

Say it with me: *Kore wa ikura? Kore, kudasai. Hai. Iie.*

Try saying them like you're in a real store. Yes, you can pretend you're holding a rice ball. It helps.

Kanji of the Day: 円

- **Meaning:** Yen / Circle
- **Reading:** えん (*en*)
- **Mnemonic:** Think of a box—square, simple, and valuable. It looks like a box enclosing something inside.

You'll see this everywhere in Japan:

- On price tags
- In restaurant menus
- On vending machines
- At ATMs
- In anime subtitles, whenever money is involved

This one kanji instantly unlocks your ability to understand prices.

Stroke Order

1. Horizontal top stroke
2. Short vertical inside
3. Closing box around the bottom (written like a frame)

Try this: Draw it once big, once medium, once small. Say "*en*" each time you finish.

Mini-Dialogue: Buying Something in a Store

A: これはいくら? (*Ko-re wa i-ku-ra?* – How much is this?)

B: 千円です。(*Sen en de-su.* – It's 1,000 yen.)

A: これ、ください。(*Ko-re, ku-da-sai.* – This, please.)

B: はい。ありがとうございます。(*Ha-i. A-ri-ga-tou go-zai-ma-su.* – Yes. Thank you very much.)

Try plugging in different prices you've heard:

- 五百円 (*go-hyaku en*) – 500 yen
- 二千円 (*ni-sen en*) – 2,000 yen

Don't worry about mastering large numbers today. Focus on the flow of the dialogue and understanding 円 as the money marker.

Cultural Insight: Japan Is a Cash Society

In Japan, especially outside major cities, cash is king. Many small shops don't accept cards. You'll also notice that bills are often crisp and clean, people handle their money carefully, even placing it on trays rather than directly into someone's hand.

- **Anime Moment:** In *Sailor Moon,* you'll often see characters shopping with coins, grabbing street snacks, or running errands for their moms. It's casual, and usually done with pocket change.

- **Travel Tip:** Keep small bills and coins with you—especially ¥1,000 and ¥500. Use "これはいくら?" (*ko-re wa i-ku-ra?*) if a price isn't visible, and always say "ありがとうございます" (*a-ri-ga-tou-go-zai-ma-su*) when you pay.

Quick Quiz – 1 Minute

1. What does "これ、ください" mean?
   a. How much is this?
   b. This, please
   c. I don't want this
2. Which phrase means "yes"?
   a. はい
   b. いいえ
   c. こんにちは
3. What is the kanji for yen?
   a. 一
   b. 人
   c. 円

Bonus Challenge: Look at something on your desk or nearby. Pretend you're in a Japanese store and say: "これはいくら?" (*ko-re wa i-ku-ra?*) then "これ、ください。" (*Ko-re, ku-da-sai*). Say it out loud!

Answers: 1–b, 2–a, 3–c

XP Earned: 20

You just unlocked the power to buy things like a local. That's huge.

Badge Progress: Phrase Pioneer – 4/5 Days Complete. You're almost at your first badge—keep it going!

Final Thoughts

Being able to ask "How much is this?" might seem basic, but it's the difference between watching Japan and actually experiencing it.

When you walk into a shop and confidently say, "*Kore wa ikura?*" instead of fumbling or pointing awkwardly, something shifts. You're now a communicator.

And communication—however simple—is powerful.

Let's wrap up Week 1 strong. See you for Day 5!

Scan to Listen

13%.....Complete!!

Day 5: The Magic of Japanese Sentences

05

Mission: Discover Why Japanese Sentences Sound So Different

Look at you.

In just five days, you've gone from "*I've always wanted to learn Japanese...*" to actually using it—greeting people, making polite requests, asking questions, and even recognizing your first kanji.

Today, you're unlocking one of the most fascinating things about Japanese: how its sentences are built. Spoiler: They don't work like English ones.

In fact, they often feel backward at first. But once you get it? Everything clicks.

English vs. Japanese: Why the Word Order Feels So Wild

Let's start with this sentence:

English: I eat sushi.

Japanese: わたしは すしを たべます。(*Wa-ta-shi wa su-shi o ta-be-ma-su.*)

See the difference?

In English, the word order is: → Subject + Verb + Object → "I eat sushi."

But in Japanese, it flips to: → Subject + Object + Verb → "I sushi eat."

And the secret? Those little particles like は (*wa*) and を (*o*). Think of them as signposts that tell you what role each word plays, regardless of where it shows up in the sentence.

Let's try a few more!

Sentence Switch Challenge

Match the parts and see how the structure flows:

- これを (*kor-e o*) = this [object marker]
- のみます (*no-mi-ma-su*) = drink
- わたしは (*wa-ta-shi wa*) = I [topic marker]

Full Sentence: わたしは これを のみます。(*Wa-ta-shi wa ko-re o no-mi-ma-su*).

Translation: *I drink this.*

Literal: *I this drink.*

See how the verb always comes at the end? That's one of the key patterns of Japanese, and why it can feel surprising at first.

Why This Matters

Once you start thinking in Japanese order, it gets easier to:

- Understand what you're hearing (especially in anime or conversations).
- Build your own sentences faster.
- Avoid direct, awkward translations from English.

Instead of translating word-for-word, you're now learning to feel the flow of Japanese.

Quick Primer: What Are "Particles" in Japanese?

Japanese sentences rely heavily on particles. These are tiny words that come after nouns, verbs, or other parts of a sentence to show what role each part plays. English uses word order and prepositions. Japanese uses these particles instead.

Let's look at a few of the most common ones you'll learn:

Particle	Written As	Pronounced As	Function	Example
は	*wa*	*wa*	Topic marker ("as for…")	わたしは グレースです。 *Wa-ta-shi wa Grace de-su.* As for me, I'm Grace.
を	*o*	*o*	Direct object marker (what's being acted on)	パンを たべます。 *Pan o ta-be-ma-su.* I eat bread.
に	*ni*	*ni*	Indicates direction, time, or destination	学校に 行きます。 *Ga-kkou ni i-ki-ma-su.* I go to school.
で	*de*	*de*	Indicates where an action takes place	レストランで たべます。 *Re-su-to-ran de ta-be-ma-su.* I eat at a restaurant.

の	*no*	*no*	Possession / “of” / belonging	せんせいの ほんです。 *Sen-sei no hon de-su.* It’s the teacher’s book.
と	*to*	*to*	“And” / “with”	ともだちと はなします。 *To-mo-da-chi to ha-na-shi-ma-su.* I talk with my friend.

You’ll see these pop up every day, and I’ll break them down naturally through conversation practice. Think of particles as the invisible string that ties a sentence together.

Build a Sentence (Your Turn!)

Let’s use some of your phrases from this week.

Try building: “I want this.” Hint:

- わたしは (*wa-ta-shi wa*) = I
- これが (*ko-re ga*) = this [subject marker for desire]
- ほしいです (*ho-shii de-su*) = want

Answer: わたしは これが ほしいです。(Literally: I this want.)

Want to say “Please give me that”? You already know this one: それをください。(*So-re o ku-da-sai.* – That, please.)

The structure may feel inside out at first, but your brain will adjust. Trust it.

Cultural Insight: Speaking in Circles (and Why That's Not Bad)

Japanese favors indirectness and grace. Instead of blunt statements, sentences flow like a river—smooth, with intention. That's why subjects are often dropped when obvious. That's why verbs end thoughts softly.

In English, we get straight to the point. In Japanese, we often circle the meaning, out of respect and subtlety.

Learning to enjoy that rhythm will help you sound more natural and connect more.

Mini Practice Quiz – Sentence Detective

What's the correct Japanese order?

1. "I read this."
    a. わたしe よみます これを
    b. わたしは これを よみます
    c. これを わたしは よみます
2. Which part means "object"?
    a. を
    b. は
    c. が
3. "This, please."
    a. これ、ください
    b. ください、これ
    c. これを、ください

Answers: 1-b, 2-a, c-a

XP Earned: 20

You finished your first full week! Time to celebrate that brain of yours.

Badge Earned: Phrase Pioneer

You've completed 5 days, learned 8+ phrases, 5 kanji, and survived your first Japanese dialogues. That's not just beginner status; that's beginning mastery.

Week 1: Gem of Connection

Oh! What's this?

You've taken your first steps in a whole new language—and more importantly, you've already done what most never do: you began.

This gem represents the spark of human connection; the moment a word becomes a doorway to understanding. You've learned to greet, thank, and introduce yourself with sincerity and clarity. That's no small thing.

Gem of Connection Earned

Mark your tracker. You're 1/5 of the way there. Keep going!

Final Thoughts

This week, you started reshaping your brain to think in a brand-new pattern.

That's more than learning. That's rewiring.

Next week, we'll put this sentence knowledge to work in real-life situations: ordering food, asking for directions, and more.

But for now? Breathe. You're doing this.

See you in Week 2!

Scan to Listen

16%.....Complete!!

Personal Phrase Journal

Language is more than vocabulary. It's not just what you say. It's how it feels to say it.

This will let you remember the moments that mattered: the phrase that made you smile, the word you whispered with confidence, the kanji that suddenly made sense.

Over the next six weeks, you'll use these pages to slow down and reflect on your journey: What you've learned, how you've grown, and what feels most like you. Because fluency isn't just about grammar or tests. It's about expression. Connection. Ownership.

Here's your space to do just that. Collect the words that feel like home. Write the phrases that sound like you. Celebrate what no app or textbook can track: your voice, your growth, and your courage to keep going.

Week 1: Foundations of Japanese Interaction

Focus: Getting comfortable, celebrating firsts, choosing favorite words.

My Favorite Phrase This Week

Japanese: ______________________________

Romaji: ______________________________

English: ______________________________

What about this phrase made it stick for me?

____

____

____

A Moment I Felt Brave Saying Something

What did I say or try? Where was I? How did it feel?

- ❑ Fun
- ❑ Scary
- ❑ Empowering
- ❑ Awkward
- ❑ Exciting

Reflection:

____

____

____

New Words That Feel Like Me

- ____
  - » Why: ____
- ____
  - » Why: ____

A Phrase That Made Me Smile

Phrase: ____

Why: ____

Next Week's Intention

- ❑ Say a phrase in real life
- ❑ Try a full sentence
- ❑ Rewatch a scene in Japanese
- ❑ Other: ____

Week 2: Facing Daily Life

Close your eyes for a second and picture this: You're standing at a Tokyo train station. Announcements echo overhead. People rush past in crisp uniforms and headphones. You spot a noodle shop tucked in the corner, and it smells incredible. A tiny voice in your head says, "You can do this."

This is the week when your Japanese starts feeling real.

Last week, you built your foundation: greetings, requests, and your first five kanjis. Now, we're stepping into daily life in Japan—how to get around, ask for help, buy a train ticket, order at a restaurant, or ask someone where the restroom is without resorting to wild gestures and panic-eyes.

These are survival skills. And more than that, they're tools for freedom.

Because when you can say things like "Where's the station?" or "Can I get some water, please?" you stop feeling like a tourist and start feeling like a traveler. You're connecting. You're living in the language.

What You'll Learn This Week

This week, you'll learn:

- How to ask for directions (and understand the answers!).

- How to ride public transportation without confusion.
- How to order food at a restaurant like a pro.
- How to express basic needs and emergencies.
- How to say "I don't understand" (and stay calm while doing it).
- New kanji for places, movement, and support.
- Real-life phrases pulled from train stations, restaurants, and anime.

Why This Week Matters

Week 1 taught you how to start a conversation. Week 2 teaches you how to keep going.

We're moving from fixed phrases to flexible language, from scripted to situational. The kind of language that keeps you calm when the train schedule changes. That helps you politely ask for help when you're lost. That lets you order ramen with a smile and actually understand the response.

So grab your (imaginary) train pass. We're about to step into Japan's daily life.

Your next stop? Ask for directions.

Let's go.

Day 6: Ask for Directions

06

Mission: Find Your Way—Without Feeling Lost

Let's set the scene: You've just stepped off the train in a new part of town. The streets are buzzing, the vending machines are glowing, and your phone's GPS? Yeah, it just lost signal. You glance around, spotting a friendly-looking local.

You walk up, smile, and say:

"すみません、えきはどこですか?" (*Su-mi-ma-sen, e-ki wa do-ko-de-su ka?* / Excuse me, where's the station?)

Boom. You just connected. You didn't panic. You didn't fumble. You asked like a local.

Today's mission is simple but powerful: Learn how to ask for directions, and understand the basics of the answer. No stress. No complicated grammar. Just one step closer to navigating Japan with confidence.

Phrases of the Day

Japanese	Pronunciation	Meaning
どこですか?	*do-ko de-su ka?*	Where is it?
えきはどこですか?	*e-ki wa do-ko de-su ka?*	Where's the station?
みぎ	*mi-gi*	Right
ひだり	*hi-da-ri*	Left

How to Use Them

- どこですか? ***(Do-ko-de-su ka?)*** means "Where is it?" Use it after naming any place or object.
- えきはどこですか? ***(E-ki wa do-ko-de-su ka?)*** means "Where's the station?" But you can replace "えき" with any place:
    - » トイレはどこですか? (*To-ire wa do-ko de-su ka?* – Where's the restroom?)
    - » コンビニはどこですか? (*Kon-bi-ni wa do-ko de-su ka?* – Where's the convenience store?)
- みぎ ***(mi-gi)*** = Right
- ひだり ***(hi-da-ri)*** = Left

Practice out loud: "すみません、えきはどこですか?" (*Su-mi-ma-sen, e-ki wa do-ko-de-su ka?*). If that flows smoothly, you're already ahead of the game.

Kanji of the Day: 駅

- **Meaning:** Station.
- **Reading:** えき (*e-ki*).
- **Mnemonic:** Picture a horse arriving at a stop. Long ago, stations were places where riders changed horses.

This kanji is all over Japan:

- On maps
- At train platforms
- In subway apps
- Even in anime episode titles involving travel

Once you recognize 駅, you'll never get totally lost.

Stroke Order

1. Radical on the left = horse (a hint of tradition)
2. Right-hand parts = stop/structure

Write it out once—even if it's messy. This one's your new travel buddy.

Mini-Dialogue: Getting Directions

A: すみません、えきはどこですか？（*Su-mi-ma-sen, e-ki wa do-ko-de-su ka?* – Excuse me, where's the station?)

B: みぎです。(*Mi-gi de-su.* – It's to the right.)

A: ありがとうございます！（*A-ri-ga-tou go-zai-ma-su!* – Thank you very much!)

Want more details? You might hear:

- "まっすぐです" (*ma-ssu-gu de-su*) – Go straight.
- "かどをひだりです"（*ka-do o hi-da-ri de-su*) – Turn left at the corner. But don't worry about that today. You're learning the essentials—and that's enough.

Cultural Insight: Ask First, Point Second

In Japan, it's common—and appreciated—to ask for help politely. People are usually more than willing to assist, especially when you lead with "すみません" (*sumimasen*) and speak clearly.

Many locals will even walk you part of the way if they notice you're lost.

- **Anime Moment:** In *Attack on Titan,* characters often reference locations—"地下室はどこ?"（*Chi-ka-shi-tsu wa do-ko?* / Where's the basement?) during moments of urgency. But even in calm slice-of-life anime, you'll notice students asking for directions at school or while exploring town.

- **Travel Tip:** Add a slight bow when asking. Don't be afraid to use gestures alongside your Japanese. Pointing at your map or looking curious is totally normal and often leads to new connections.

Quick Quiz – 1 Minute

1. What does "どこですか?" (*do-ko-de-su ka*) mean?

    a. What is it?

    b. Where is it?

    c. How much is it?

2. What does "ひだり" (*hi-da-ri*) mean?

    a. Right

    b. Left

    c. Back

3. What kanji means "station"?

    a. 駅

    b. 円

    c. 人

Bonus Challenge: Look up a place in your town (like a coffee shop) and say: "[Place name] はどこですか?" ([Place name] *Wa do-ko-de-su ka?*). Try it out loud!

Answers: 1–b, 2–b, 3–a

XP Earned: 20

Look at you, asking questions like a pro.

Badge Progress: Travel Trailblazer – 1/5 Days Complete. Just a few more steps and you'll unlock your second badge!

Final Thoughts

Today, you learned how to find your way without needing perfect grammar, advanced vocabulary, or a translation app.

You asked. You listened. You understood. And if that's not real-world fluency in motion, I don't know what is.

So next time you're exploring, even if it's just a new aisle in your grocery store, practice asking "Where is...?" with confidence.

Because you're not getting lost anymore. You're finding your way in Japanese.

Tomorrow, we take that same confidence to the train station. Let's ride the rails with public transport.

Ready to board?

Scan to Listen

20%.....Complete!!

Day 7: Public Transport

07

Mission: Ride Like a Local

If you ever visit Japan, you'll notice something right away: The public transportation system works. It's clean, on time, and so quiet you can hear your own thoughts.

But when you're the one trying to figure out what ticket to buy or which train is going where? It can feel like decoding a puzzle··· in another language.

Today's mission? Learn how to ask about tickets, times, and trains. You'll also get a new kanji you'll see on every subway platform in Japan. After this, the next time you step onto a platform, you'll know what to say and what to look for.

Let's hop on.

Phrases of the Day

Japanese	Pronunciation	Meaning
いくらですか?	*i-ku-ra de-su ka?*	How much is it?
きっぷ	*ki-ppu*	Ticket
なんじ?	*nan-ji?*	What time?
でんしゃ	*den-sha*	Train

How to Use Them

- **いくらですか? "How much is it?"**: You learned "これ、いくら?" (*ko-re, i-ku-ra?*), before—this version is more general. Add it to specific words, like:
  - » きっぷは、いくらですか? (*Ki-ppu wa, i-ku-ra-de-su ka?*) – How much is the ticket?

- **きっぷ = Ticket:** You'll see this at machines and booths. Easy to remember: sounds a little like "coupon."
- **なんじ? = What time?** This is a simple, informal way to ask for the time. Great to pair with pointing at a sign or clock.
- **でんしゃ = Train:** This is the generic word for "train." There are more specific types (express, local, etc.), but this one works in 95% of situations.

Practice saying: "きっぷ、いくらですか?" "なんじに でんしゃ が きますか?" (*Ki-ppu, i-ku-ra-de-su ka? Nan-ji ni den-sha ga ki-ma-su ka?*).

Don't worry if that second one is tricky. Even just asking "なんじ?" (*Nan-ji?*), while pointing is enough to get help.

Kanji of the Day: 車

- **Meaning:** Vehicle / Car / Train
- **Reading:** くるま (*ku-ru-ma*) or しゃ (*sha*)
- **Mnemonic:** Looks like a bird's-eye view of a vehicle, big wheel in the middle, axles around it.

You'll see this kanji in words like:

- 自転車 (*ji-ten-sha*) – bicycle
- 電車 (*den-sha*) – train (electric vehicle)
- 車 (*ku-ru-ma*) – car

You already know this one from でんしゃ! (*Den-sha!*)

Stroke Order

1. Box on top
2. Middle vertical line
3. Horizontal lines inside and below

Write it 3x and whisper "*sha... sha... sha.*" Yep—it's weird, but it works.

Mini-Dialogue: Asking for a Train Ticket

A: すみません、きっぷは いくらですか？（*Su-mi-ma-sen, ki-ppu wa i-ku-ra de-su ka?* – Excuse me, how much is the ticket?)

B: にひゃくえんです。（*Ni-hya-ku en de-su.* – It's 200 yen.)

A: ありがとうございます！（*A-ri-ga-tou go-zai-ma-su!* – Thank you very much!)

Add-on phrase if you're feeling bold: なんじに でんしゃが きますか？（*Nan-ji ni den-sha ga ki-ma-su ka?* – What time does the train come?)

Even if the answer goes over your head, just listening helps you grow.

Cultural Insight: Train Etiquette 101

Japanese trains are efficient, silent, and deeply respectful. You won't hear loud phone calls or see people eating. Instead, you'll see people reading, sleeping, or quietly scrolling their phones.

Train stations are also full of signs, arrows, ticket machines, and maps—in Japanese. That's where today's phrases save the day.

- **Anime Moment:** In *Spirited Away,* Chihiro rides a mysterious train across a quiet sea. No announcements. No distractions. Just the steady rhythm of motion. That's the vibe in real life, too. Calming. Ordered. Peaceful.
- **Travel Tip:** If you're unsure what train to take, go to the ticket counter and say:
    - » すみません、[Destination]　まで、きっぷ　ください。（*Su-mi-ma-sen,* [destination] *ma-de, ki-ppu ku-da-sai* / Excuse me, a ticket to [place], please.)

They'll usually point to a machine or give you the correct fare.

Quick Quiz – 1 Minute

1. What does "きっぷ" mean?
    a. Train
    b. Ticket
    c. Station
2. What does "なんじ?" mean?
    a. What time?
    b. Which station?
    c. How far?
3. What kanji means "vehicle"?
    a. 駅
    b. 車
    c. 円

Bonus Challenge: Try saying aloud: "でんしゃは、なんじ?" (*Nan-ji ni den-sha ga ki-ma-su ka?*)– "What time is the train?"

Answers: 1–b, 2–a, 3–b

XP Earned: 20

You just leveled up your urban survival skills.

Badge Progress: Travel Trailblazer – 2/5 Days Complete. The trains are yours now. No more confusion at the platform.

Final Thoughts

This lesson was about independence.

Now, when someone hands you a ticket, when a train announcement plays, or when a price flashes on a screen, you'll hear more than just noise. You'll hear meaning. You'll recognize sounds. You'll have options.

That's what real learning looks like—small wins that make a big difference.

Tomorrow, we're heading to the best part of Japanese life: food. Let's get ready to order meals, ask for water, and finally say "Oishii!" like we mean it.

See you for Day 8.

Ready to feast?

Scan to Listen

23%.....Complete!!

Day 8: Order Food

08

Mission: Eat Well—and Order With Confidence

Ordering food in Japanese is one of the most rewarding language wins you'll ever have.

Seriously—there's nothing like looking up from a steaming bowl of ramen, realizing you ordered it, in Japanese, and the person behind the counter understood you perfectly.

That first "*Oishii!*" hits different when it comes after real interaction.

Today's mission: You'll learn how to ask for water, order a menu item, and show appreciation—three super practical phrases that will serve you everywhere from street food stalls to izakaya pubs to fancy sushi bars.

Phrases of the Day

Japanese	Pronunciation	Meaning
メニューをください	*men-yuu o ku-da-sai*	Menu, please
みずをください	*mi-zu o ku-da-sai*	Water, please
おいしい	*oi-shii*	Delicious!
ごちそうさまでした	*go-chisou-sama -deshi-ta*	Thank you for the meal (after eating)

How to Use Them

- ***メニューをください (men-yuu o ku-da-sai)***: Walk into any restaurant and say this—politely and with a smile. The server will bring you a menu (and probably appreciate your effort!).

- **みずをください *(mi-zu o ku-da-sai)***: Want a glass of water? Say this. Japanese restaurants often serve free water or tea, but it's still polite to ask. Say "すみません" first to get someone's attention.
- **おいしい!*(oi-shii)***: One of the most joyful words in the language. Say it mid-meal or after your first bite. It's the ultimate food compliment.
- **ごちそうさまでした *(go-chisou-sama -deshi-ta)***: A phrase packed with gratitude. You say it after eating, to thank the cook/server for the meal, even if you're alone. It's respectful and very Japanese.

Try this: Say "おいしい!" (*oi-shii*) like you just had the best bite of your life. Then follow it up with "ごちそうさまでした" (*go-chisou-sama -deshi-ta*) in a calm and contented voice.

Kanji of the Day: 食 and 水

食

- **Reading:** しょく (*sho-ku*) or たべ (*ta-be*)
- **Meaning:** Eat
- **Mnemonic:** Imagine a person at a table, ready to eat. The kanji looks like a lid over a bowl of food.

水

- **Reading:** みず (*mi-zu*)
- **Meaning:** Water
- **Mnemonic:** Flowing strokes that look like drops of water or a stream.

You'll find these in:

- 食べます (*ta-be-ma-su*) – to eat
- 食堂 (*sho-ku-dou*) – cafeteria
- 飲食 (*in-sh-oku*) – food and drink

- 水曜日 (*sui-you-bi*) – Wednesday (literally: water day!)
- 水道 (*sui-dou*) – water supply

Stroke Order

食

1. Top-down roof
2. Vertical and cross strokes under it

水

1. Central line with flowing branches like water streaming down.

Write each once. Say "たべる" (*ta-be-ru*) when you write 食, and "みず" (*mi-zu*) when you write 水.

Mini-Dialogue: At the Restaurant

A: すみません、メニューをください。(*Su-mi-ma-sen, me-nyuu o ku-da-sai.* – Excuse me, menu please.)

B: はい、どうぞ。(*Hai, dou-zo.* – Sure, here you go.)

A: みずをください。(*Mi-zu o ku-da-sai.* – Water, please.)

B: はい。(*Hai.* – Okay.)

A: おいしい！(*Oi-shii!* – Delicious!)

A: ごちそうさまでした。(*Go-chi-sou-sa-ma de-shi-ta.* – Thank you for the meal.)

Try practicing this as a full role-play, even if it's just you and your reflection. Better yet, practice it while eating something good!

Cultural Insight: Food Is a Conversation

In Japan, ordering food is about more than just feeding yourself; it's about showing respect.

You'll rarely hear people yelling or calling across the room. Instead, they wait for eye contact, say "すみません," (*su-mi-ma-sen*), and speak softly but clearly. The meal itself is often quiet, and the phrases before and after— "いただきます" (*i-ta-da-ki-ma-su*) before eating and "ごちそうさまでした" (*Go-chisou-sama-deshi-ta*) (after)—are as important as the food.

- **Anime Moment:** In *Food Wars* (Shokugeki no Soma), characters say "おいしい!" (*Oi-shii!*) with such intensity, you'd think the food gave them a spiritual awakening. And honestly? Sometimes it feels like that.
- **Travel Tip:** Always say "ごちそうさまでした" (*Go-chi-sou-sa-ma de-shi-ta*) when you leave a restaurant, even if no one is looking. It's a small gesture that shows big respect.

Quick Quiz – 1 Minute

1. What does "みずをください" (*Mi-zu o ku-da-sai*) mean?

   a. The water is good.

   b. Give me water, please.

   c. I don't want water.

2. What's the meaning of "ごちそうさまでした" (*go-chisou-sama -deshi-ta*)?

   a. Please.

   b. Where is it?

   c. Thank you for the meal.

3. What kanji means "eat"?

   a. 食

   b. 水

   c. 円

Bonus Challenge: Say "おいしい!" (*oi-shii!*) in the mirror with emotion. Try to mean it—even if you're holding a cracker.

Answers: 1–b, 2–c, 3–a

XP Earned: 20

You've just unlocked your *foodie fluency starter kit.*

Badge Progress: Travel Trailblazer – 3/5 Days Complete. You're three meals away from feeling like a Tokyo regular.

Final Thoughts

Ordering food is a moment of joy. It's that feeling of being seen, heard, and understood in a completely new language.

You just learned how to step into a restaurant, order with confidence, and express delight clearly, politely, and naturally.

And tomorrow? You'll learn how to ask for help. From finding the restroom to saying "I don't understand" without freezing up.

Let's keep going. You've got this.

See you for Day 9!

Scan to Listen

26%.....Complete!!

Day 9: Express Needs

09

Mission: Ask for Help Without Panic

Let's face it—sometimes things go sideways.

Your phone dies. You can't find the restroom. You miss a stop. Or someone speaks too fast and you just··· blank. We've all been there.

But here's the secret: You don't need perfect grammar to handle it. You just need a few clear, calm phrases—and the confidence to use them.

Today's mission is all about asking for help, clarifying confusion, and keeping cool in unexpected situations. Because fluency isn't just about talking; it's about asking when you don't know what to say.

Phrases of the Day

Japanese	Pronunciation	Meaning
トイレはどこですか?	*toi-re wa do-ko de-su ka?*	Where's the bathroom?
たすけて!	*ta-su-ke-te!*	Help!
わかりません	*wa-ka-ri-ma-sen*	I don't understand
ゆっくり ください	*yu-kku-ri ku-da-sai*	Please speak slowly

How to Use Them

- **トイレはどこですか?**: Let's be honest: This is one of the most important phrases in any language. Learn it. Use it. Say it with a smile and a slightly desperate tone, and you'll get help fast.

- **たすけて!:** This is your emergency word. Say it loudly and clearly if you ever need real help. It's strong, so don't use it lightly—but it's there for you if needed.
- **わかりません:** Polite, clear, and humble. Say this when someone speaks too fast or you're simply lost. Follow it up with a smile or gesture, and most people will slow down or try again.
- **ゆっくり ください:** Literally "slowly, please." You can also say "ゆっくり おねがいします" (*"Yu-kku-ri o-ne-gai shi-ma-su"*) for more formality. Works wonders in conversations, shops, or at a train station.

Practice: Say "わかりません" (*wa-ka-ri-ma-sen*) in a calm, kind voice. Then say "ゆっくり、ください" (*yu-kku-ri ku-da-sai*) like you're kindly asking someone to slow down without shame. Because it's totally okay to need that.

Kanji of the Day: 助

- **Meaning:** Help
- **Reading:** たす (*ta-su-ke*), じょ (*jo*)
- **Mnemonic:** Picture two hands reaching out, powered by strength. Helping hands with energy.

You'll see it in:

- 助ける (*ta-su-ke-ru*) – to help
- 救助 (*kyuu-jo*) – rescue
- 助手 (*jo-shu*) – assistant

It's a kanji that reminds you: You're allowed to need help, and to give it too.

Stroke Order

1. Left radical: 力 (power)
2. Right components: hand + support strokes

Write it once while saying "たすけて." (*ta-su-ke-te*). Let your hand remember the shape.

Mini-Dialogue: Asking for Help

A: すみません、トイレはどこですか? (*Su-mi-ma-sen, toi-re wa do-ko de-su ka?* – Excuse me, where's the bathroom?)

B: あそこです。(*A-so-ko de-su.* – Over there.)

A: ありがとうございます! (*A-ri-ga-tou go-zai-ma-su!* – Thank you very much.)

Later...

A: わかりません。ゆっくり、ください。 (*Wa-ka-ri-ma-sen. Yu-kku-ri, ku-da-sai.* – I don't understand. Please speak slowly.)

B: はい、だいじょうぶです。(*Hai, dai-jou-bu de-su.* – Sure, no problem.)

Even this short exchange builds trust, and most people will meet your effort with kindness.

Cultural Insight: In Japan, It's Okay to Ask

In Japanese culture, humility is respected. Admitting you don't understand or asking for help isn't seen as a weakness. It's seen as honest and thoughtful.

And when you try—even with broken grammar or imperfect pronunciation—people often respond with extra kindness, patience, and sometimes even awe that you're learning their language.

- **Anime Moment:** In *One Piece,* Luffy's loud "たすけて!" (*ta-su-kete!*) moments are legendary, but so are his moments of confusion. "わかんねえ…" (*Wa-ka-nee…*/I don't get it…) pops up regularly, and it's relatable!
- **Travel Tip:** You'll find "トイレ" (*toi-re*) signs in train stations, restaurants, and convenience stores. If you're

ever truly lost, approach someone and say "すみません、わかりません…" (*Su-mi-ma-sen, wa-ka-ri-ma-sen...*), you'll usually be met with a helpful smile and a helpful hand.

Quick Quiz – 1 Minute

1. What does "たすけて！" mean?
   a. I'm tired
   b. Help
   c. Please eat
2. What's the polite way to say "I don't understand"?
   a. わかります
   b. わかりません
   c. しりません
3. Which kanji means "help"?
   a. 助
   b. 食
   c. 人

Bonus Challenge: Say "ゆっくり、ください" (*yu-kku-ri ku-da-sai*) slowly enough to match its meaning. That's the trick!

Answers: 1–b, 2–b, 3–a

XP Earned: 20

You've just added *life-saving language* to your tool kit.

Badge Progress: Travel Trailblazer – 4/5 Days Complete. Just one more mission and the badge is yours!

Final Thoughts

Today wasn't flashy; it was real.

You learned how to ask for help, express confusion, and slow things down. These are what keep conversations going when things get hard. And that's what fluency actually looks like.

So be proud. You've learned how to speak up, even when you don't know the words.

See you for Day 10. You've earned it.

Scan to Listen

30%.....Complete!!

Day 10: How One Phrase Can Say Ten Different Things

10

Mission: Discover How Tone and Context Shape Japanese

You made it. Not just through two weeks of lessons but through real situations, emotions, and conversations. You've asked for help. You've ordered food. You've navigated public spaces in a totally different language. That's not "beginner Japanese." That's living Japanese.

Today, let's explore something even important: How does one phrase change depending on who you're talking to, how you feel, or where you are?

Welcome to the world of contextual Japanese, where what you say is only half the message. The *how, when,* and *to whom?* That's where the magic happens.

Same Phrase, Different Feeling

Let's take a simple phrase: "わかりません" (*wa-ka-ri-ma-sen* – I don't understand)

Depending on your tone and the situation, it can mean…

Situation	Meaning	Emotion
In class	*I didn't understand that grammar point.*	Curious, focused
In a conversation	*I didn't catch what you said.*	Polite, apologetic
When you're overwhelmed	*I'm totally lost right now.*	Nervous, frustrated

With a friend	*What the heck are you talking about?!*	Playful, teasing
In an argument	*I don't get you.*	Sharp, confrontational

Same phrase. Different vibe. This is one of the biggest differences between English and Japanese. Japanese relies heavily on tone, body language, and context to convey intent.

Why This Matters in Real Life

When you're in Japan—or watching anime—you'll notice:

- People drop subjects (like "I" or "you") because the context makes it obvious.
- The same sentence can be warm or cold depending on how it's said.
- Politeness levels (like です (*de-su*) vs. だ (*da*) vs. nothing at all) signal your relationship to the person.

Knowing this makes your Japanese feel real, not robotic.

Mini Training: One Phrase, Many Ways

Let's try one more: "おいしい!" (*Oi-shii* – Delicious!)

Try saying it:

- Genuinely happy (you love the food!)
- Quietly (in a fancy restaurant)
- Exaggerated (like on a cooking show)
- Sarcastic (it's... actually bad)
- Grateful (a friend made it for you)

Each one carries a different message, and Japanese speakers pick up on these instantly.

Cultural Insight: Reading the Air (空気を読む – *kuu-ki wo yo-mu*)

Japanese people often talk about "reading the air," which means picking up on unspoken cues. In conversation, it's not just what you say, but how you tune into the room.

This is why tone matters so much. It's also why learning to speak too literally or too flatly can make you sound stiff, even if your grammar is perfect.

Anime Moment: In anime, emotional expression is turned up to max. Listen closely, and you'll hear how characters use the same words differently depending on their mood or relationship.

Examples:

"だいじょうぶ" (*Dai-jou-bu* – I'm fine)

- Said with a smile? Brave.
- Said with tears? Hiding pain.
- Yelled? A last stand.

Start mimicking not just what your favorite characters say, but how they say it.

Quick Quiz – Feel the Difference

1. Which "わかりません" would feel rude in a polite situation?

    a. Soft tone, apologetic face

    b. Blank face, flat tone

    c. Bowing slightly while speaking

2. Which of these makes you sound friendly in a restaurant?

    a. おいしい! with a big smile

    b. おいしい。with a deadpan face

    c. Saying nothing and just nodding politely

3. What does "reading the air" mean in Japan?
    a. Checking the weather
    b. Guessing people's feelings and acting accordingly
    c. Listening for background music to set the mood

Reflection Prompt: What emotions do you want your Japanese to carry? Kindness? Curiosity? Confidence? Can you think of a moment when tone changed the meaning of what someone said to you?

Answers: 1-b, 2-a, 3-b

XP Earned: 20

Congratulations—you've completed Week 2!

Badge Earned: Travel Trailblazer

You've mastered everyday navigation, food, transport, and asking for help. You're officially capable of handling real-life situations in Japanese.

Week 2: Gem of Curiosity

You've made it through your second week, and with it, you've unlocked one of the most powerful tools a language learner can have: curiosity.

This week, you asked questions, made polite requests, and explored the cultural heartbeat behind the language.

Gem of Curiosity Earned

Curiosity turns confusion into progress. And you've got it.

Final Thoughts

You've learned how to speak. Now, you're learning how to be heard.

Next week, we enter a new world—anime, games, and pop culture—where rules bend, slang flies, and emotion leads the way.

You're not just saying the words. You're feeling them. And that makes you unstoppable.

See you in Week 3.

Scan to Listen

33%.....Complete!!

Personal Phrase Journal

Week 2: Facing Daily Life

Focus: Everyday use, emotions, real-life connection.

Phrase That Helped Me Connect

Phrase: ______________________________

Where did I use or imagine using it?

____

____

____

This Phrase Surprised Me

Japanese: ______________________________

Romaji: ______________________________

Why?

____

____

____

Kanji I Recognized in the Wild

Kanji: ______________________________

Where I saw it: ______________________________

What it meant to me: ______________________________

Next Week's Intention

- ❏ Read a menu or a sign
- ❏ Speak 3 phrases in a row
- ❏ Use a new kanji
- ❏ Other: ______________________________

Week 3: Anime and Pop Culture

Learn the Language You Fell in Love With

Let's be real: for many of us, anime was the spark.

That one scene where a character yells "*Ganbare!*" with tears in their eyes. The moment someone whispers "*Daijoubu*" to comfort a friend. The jokes that hit even harder when you understand just one word without subtitles.

This week is about that spark.

You're going to learn how to speak like your favorite anime characters—not in over-the-top ways (well, maybe a little)—but in ways that are fun, expressive, and emotionally rich.

These are the words fans around the world learn first, because they make you feel like you belong in the story.

And the best part? Many of these words are actually used in everyday Japanese, especially among friends, peers, and young people. So while they're fun and sometimes dramatic, they're also real.

This week is going to boost your confidence, expand your emotional expression, and connect you with the reason you started learning in the first place.

What You'll Learn This Week

This week, you'll learn:

- How to greet and check in with friends using casual phrases.
- How to express feelings like happiness, sadness, and frustration.
- Common catchphrases from anime, and how to use them in real life.
- Words for love, excitement, and admiration.
- A feel for tone, energy, and cultural emotion in language.
- Kanji that reflect power, emotion, and spirit.

Why This Week Matters

Up until now, you've learned how to move through Japan, to ask, order, clarify, and respond. This week, we go deeper. We learn how to feel through Japanese, to react, relate, and connect.

These phrases let you:

- Greet friends with warmth.
- Celebrate wins (or scream when your favorite character dies).
- Express love and admiration with nuance.
- Handle casual conversations at anime conventions or online chats.
- Build emotional fluency.

You didn't sign up for this journey just to ask where the restroom is.

You came here because something about the Japanese language spoke to you. And now you get to step into that voice. Speak like the characters you love. Laugh at jokes you understand. And connect with a whole new part of yourself through sound, rhythm, and feeling.

So let's do it. Let's yell "*Yatta!*" when we get something right. Let's say "*Daijoubu?*" when a friend looks down. Let's tell someone "*Kawaii!*" when their cosplay is amazing.

And it all starts tomorrow with the words that anime friends say every time they meet: "*Yo! Genki?*"

Let's go.

Day 11: Anime Greetings

Mission: Say Hello Like a Character

You've probably heard these phrases before, shouted across school rooftops, whispered in romantic confessions, or exchanged mid-battle by best friends and rivals.

Today, you'll actually learn how to use them.

We're starting Week 3 with greetings that are casual, emotional, and anime-authentic. You'll learn how friends check in, hype each other up, and connect in a way that's warm and informal.

These phrases are real… and a little dramatic. Yes, they sound like anime (because they are), but Japanese people actually use them in everyday conversation, just with a bit less shouting.

Phrases of the Day

Japanese	Pronunciation	Meaning
よ!	*yo!*	Yo! / Hey!
げんき?	*gen-ki?*	You good? / How are you?
すごい!	*su-goi!*	Amazing! / Wow!
だいじょうぶ?	*dai-jou-bu?*	Are you okay?

How to Use Them

- よ! ***(yo!)***: Casual, short, and super friendly. Use this like you'd say "Hey!" to a friend—no need for formal greetings here.
- げんき? ***(gen-ki?)***: Informal "How are you?" Literally: "Healthy?" You can ask this when checking in on someone. Use it with friends, family, or anyone you're close to.

- すごい! ***(su-goi!)***: This one means "Awesome!" "Cool!" "Wow!" It's your all-purpose hype word—perfect for reacting to cosplay, art, food, or a plot twist.
- だいじょうぶ? ***(dai-jou-bu?)***: Means "Are you okay?" or "You alright?" Say it when someone looks upset or tired. Soft and kind.

Practice Tip: Say "げんき?" as if you're smiling. Then try "だいじょうぶ?" like you're gently checking on a friend.

Kanji of the Day: 気

- **Meaning:** Spirit / Energy / Mood
- **Reading:** き (*ki*)
- **Mnemonic:** Think of steam rising from a warm cup; your "*ki*" is what floats off your emotions, your vibe.

This kanji is in:

- 元気 (*gen-ki*) – healthy, well.
- 気持ち (*ki-mo-chi*) – feeling.
- 気をつけて (*ki o tsu-ke-te*) – take care.

Stroke Order

1. Roof-like top
2. "Rice" shape underneath (米)
3. Tail that swirls like wind

Say *"ki... ki... ki..."* while writing it out—it'll stick better that way.

Mini-Dialogue: Greeting a Friend

A: よ! げんき? (*Yo! Gen-ki?* – Hey! You good?)

B: うん、すごい! (*Un, su-goi!* – Yeah, awesome!)

A: ほんと? だいじょうぶ? (*Hon-to? Dai-jou-bu?* – Really? You okay?)

B: だいじょうぶ! ありがとう。(*Dai-jou-bu! A-ri-ga-tou.* – I'm okay! Thanks.)

Try saying this whole convo with different tones. That's how anime characters bring words to life.

Cultural Insight: Casual Talk = Real Talk

In Japan, speech shifts depending on the situation. The phrases you learned today are casual, used between friends, classmates, or people your age.

It's how characters in anime talk when they're being real. Not polite, not formal, just emotionally present.

- **Anime Moment:** In *Dragon Ball Z,* Goku often greets friends with "よ!" (*yo!*) and checks in with a casual "元気か?" (*gen-ki ga?*) His tone says: "We're close. I care." You'll hear the same vibe in *My Hero Academia, Naruto,* and nearly every school anime ever.
- **Fan Tip:** Use "よ!" (*yo!*) or "すごい!" (*su-goi!*) freely at conventions or fan events. People will know you're not just a learner; you're a fan with vocabulary.

Quick Quiz – 1 Minute

1. What does "げんき?" mean?

    a. Tired?

    b. Are you okay?

    c. Are you well?

2. What does “すごい!” mean?

    a. Hello
    b. Amazing!
    c. Later!

3. Which kanji means “spirit” or “energy”?

    a. 愛
    b. 気
    c. 力

Bonus Prompt: Text a friend “*Yo!*” in Japanese: よ! Just try it.

Answers: 1–c, 2–b, 3–b

XP Earned: 20

You just unlocked *emotional energy* in Japanese.

Badge Progress: Anime Aficionado – 1/5 Days Complete. You’re officially talking like someone from your favorite show.

Final Thoughts

This was a vibe.

You've stepped into casual conversation. You've tapped into an emotional tone. And you've started speaking like someone who doesn't just study Japanese but lives it through pop culture.

Tomorrow, we go deeper: joy, sadness, triumph, defeat. Get ready to express real feelings in Japanese.

See you for Day 12!

Scan to Listen

36%.....Complete!!

Day 12: Express Emotions

12

Mission: Feel It. Say It. Mean It.

Japanese is often described as a reserved, polite language, and that's true in formal situations. But in casual settings and anime? Emotions run wild.

One second, a character is laughing with joy, the next they're bawling dramatically or screaming "*YATTA!*" with arms in the air. And guess what?

Those words are real. Those feelings are real. And today, they're yours.

We're going to explore four powerful emotional expressions that show up in anime and real life. These aren't textbook vocabulary lists. These are the words that let you speak from the heart.

Phrases of the Day

Japanese	Pronunciation	Meaning
うれしい	*u-re-shii*	I'm happy
かなしい	*ka-na-shii*	I'm sad
やった!	*ya-tta!*	I did it! / Hooray!
だめ	*da-me*	No good / Don't do that / Not okay

How to Use Them

- **うれしい *(u-re-shii)***: Say this when something genuinely makes you happy. A good meal. Good news. A text from a friend. Just smile and say "うれしい〜."

- **かなしい *(ka-na-shii)***: Expresses sadness. It can be dramatic or heartfelt. Say it when your favorite character dies, your snack falls on the floor, or you just need to admit you're feeling low.
- **やった! *(ya-tta!)***: The victory cry of Japan. Use it for big wins (I passed!) or small ones (I found my phone!). Bonus: Say it like an anime character for full effect.
- **だめ *(da-me)***: Means "No!" or "Don't!"—but with care. Use it to stop someone gently or warn against something. Can be serious or playful depending on tone.

Try this: Say "やった!" while raising your arms like a sports anime character. Then whisper "かなしい…" like a rainy-day scene. Yes, tone matters. Drama optional. Emotion mandatory.

Kanji of the Day: 心

- **Meaning:** Heart / Feelings / Emotion
- **Reading:** こころ (*ko-ko-ro*), しん (*shin*)
- **Mnemonic:** Looks like a simplified drawing of a real heart—beating, feeling, reacting.

You'll see it in:

- 心配 (*shin-pai*) – worry
- 心 (*ko-ko-ro*) – heart/mind
- 熱心 (*ne-sshin*) – passionate
- 安心 (*an-shin*) – relief

Stroke Order

1. Top left stroke (small hook)
2. Central vertical with a curve
3. Final swoop to the right (like a flick)

Write it three times. Say "*kokoro*" each time, like you're grounding yourself in feeling.

Mini-Dialogue: Reactions with Feeling

A: プレゼント? うれしい! (*Pu-re-zen-to? U-re-shii!* – A present? I'm so happy!)

B: やったね! (*Ya-tta ne!* – You did it!)

A: でも、昨日のアニメ…かなしい。(*De-mo, ki-nou no a-ni-me... ka-na-shii.* – But yesterday's anime... was so sad.)

B: うん。だめ、ほんとに。(*Un. Da-me, hon-toni.* – Yeah. Just not okay.)

This is how real conversations happen—quick shifts between joy and frustration, love and sadness. And now you can express them in Japanese.

Cultural Insight: Japan Has Words for Quiet Feelings, Too

In Japanese, emotions are often expressed with sound and subtlety. You don't always need a full sentence, just a word and the right tone.

That's why anime is such a powerful learning tool. It exaggerates tone and body language, giving you permission to feel more fully.

- **Anime Moment:** In *Clannad,* the word "うれしい" (*u-re-shii*) breaks hearts—and heals them. In *Demon Slayer,* Tanjiro says "だめだよ" (*Da-me-da yo*) to protect someone. These aren't dramatic lines; they're sincere ones.
- **Travel Tip:** If you're watching anime or reading manga, pause when someone says "やった!" (*ya-tta*) or "かなしい..." (*ka-na-shii*) and repeat it. Match their emotion. That's how you train your instincts.

Quick Quiz – 1 Minute

1. What does "うれしい" mean?
    a. Angry
    b. Happy
    c. Surprised
2. Which phrase means "I did it!"?
    a. やった!
    b. だめ!
    c. すごい!
3. What kanji represents the heart?
    a. 気
    b. 力
    c. 心

Bonus: Try saying "うれしい!" and "かなしい…" with your own real-life story in mind. Feel it, don't fake it.

Answers: 1–b, 2–a, 3–c

XP Earned: 20

You just leveled up your *emotional fluency*. That's a BIG win.

Badge Progress: Anime Aficionado – 2/5 Days Complete. You're not just learning words; you're expressing yourself.

Final Thoughts

You've just added some of the most powerful, heartfelt words in the Japanese language to your vocabulary.

These are the phrases that help you celebrate, process, and connect—not just with anime, but with real people.

Tomorrow, you'll learn some catchphrases that fire you up, the ones that get shouted mid-battle, whispered in determination, or carved into your memory.

Get ready for Day 13!

Say it with me: やった! (*Ya-tta!*)

Scan to Listen

40%.....Complete!!

Day 13: Anime Catchphrases

Mission: Speak With Power and Passion

You know that moment right before a character wins the final battle, gets back up after being knocked down, or vows to protect their friends no matter what?

Yeah. That's this lesson.

Today's mission is all about catchphrases with conviction—the ones you hear in almost every anime, but might not realize are part of everyday Japanese, too. These are short, punchy, and emotionally charged. And while they sound epic, they're not just dramatic, they're powerful, simple Japanese phrases you can use whenever you need a boost.

Let's speak like we mean it.

Phrases of the Day

Japanese	Pronunciation	Meaning
まけない！	*ma-ke-nai!*	I won't lose!
ぜったいに！	*ze-ttai ni!*	Absolutely! / No matter what!
がんばれ！	*gan-ba-re!*	Do your best! / You got this!
しんけんだ！	*shin-ken da!*	I'm serious! / This is serious!

How to Use Them

- **まけない！** ***(ma-ke-nai!)***: Means "I won't lose!" Say it to psych yourself up, whether you're facing an exam, a workout, or a Monday. You'll hear this shouted mid-battle in 90% of shonen anime.

- **ぜったいに！ *(ze-ttai ni!)***: "No matter what." It intensifies whatever comes next. Say it alone or pair it with other words: "ぜったいに かつ！" (I'll absolutely win!)
- **がんばれ！ *(gan-ba-re!)***: Cheer someone on. It's kind, encouraging, and heartfelt. Use it with friends, coworkers, and classmates. You'll hear this at sports games, in classrooms, and in your own head when things get tough.
- **しんけんだ！ *(shin-ken da!)***: "This is serious!" Use this when you want someone to know you're not playing around—or when you're committing to something fully.

Practice Tip: Say each phrase as if you're becoming the anime protagonist. Yes, really. Feel it. Live it. Yell it if you have to. You're safe here.

Kanji of the Day: 力

- **Meaning:** Power / Strength
- **Reading:** ちから (*chi-ka-ra*)
- **Mnemonic:** Looks like a strong arm flexing—because that's exactly what it means.

You'll find it in:

- 力持ち (*chi-ka-ra-mo-chi*) – strong person
- 努力 (*do-ryo-ku*) – effort
- 能力 (*nou-ryo-ku*) – ability
- 力 (*chi-ka-ra*) – raw strength

Stroke Order

1. Downstroke for the arm
2. Curved hook underneath = muscle

Try writing it with your own strength. Say "*chikara*" with each stroke like you mean it.

Mini-Dialogue: Pre-Battle Vibes

A: がんばれ！（*Gan-ba-re!* – You got this!）

B: ありがとう。ぜったいに、まけない！（*A-ri-ga-tou. Ze-ttai ni, ma-ke-nai!* – Thanks. I won't lose, no matter what!）

A: しんけんだね。（*Shin-ken da ne.* – You're serious, huh?）

B: もちろん！（*Mo-chi-ron!* – Of course!）

Use this with friends when hyping them up, before exams, before auditions, or just before opening a bag of wasabi chips you regret later.

Cultural Insight: Japanese Spirit, Anime Style

The Japanese language has a long tradition of short, impactful phrases that reveal character. In anime, these expressions are amplified, but they come from real Japanese.

In real life, people say "がんばって" (*gan-ba-tte*) to coworkers. Students whisper "まけない" (*ma-ke-nai*) to themselves. Parents say "ぜったいにね！" (*ze-ttai ni ne!*) when promising something. These words are part of daily emotional life—anime just turns them up to 100.

- **Anime Moment:** In *Bleach, My Hero Academia, and Haikyuu!!*, catchphrases like "まけない！" (*ma-ke-nai!*) or " がんばれ！" (*gan-ba-re!*) are shouted before epic moments, but the real magic is in how often they're whispered when no one's watching.
- **Travel Tip:** Want to cheer someone on at a cosplay contest or karaoke night? Say "がんばれ！" (*gan-ba-re!*) with a smile and watch their face light up.

Quick Quiz – 1 Minute

1. What does "まけない" mean?

    a. I can't eat that

    b. I won't lose

    c. Let's go

2. Which phrase means "Absolutely!"?

    a. だいじょうぶ

    b. ぜったいに

    c. すごい

3. What kanji means "strength"?

    a. 心

    b. 気

    c. 力

Bonus: Write a short "anime speech" to yourself using any two phrases. Example: "がんばれ、自分。ぜったいに、できる!" (*Gan-ba-re, ji-bun. Ze-ttai-ni, de-ki-ru!* / Do your best, self. You can absolutely do it!)

Answers: 1–b, 2–b, 3–c

XP Earned: 20

You just added *verbal firepower* to your Japanese.

Badge Progress: Anime Aficionado – 3/5 Days Complete. You now officially speak anime battle language.

Final Thoughts

Language is more than conversation; it's conviction.

Today, you unlocked the words that power determination, spark comebacks, and shout victory. These aren't just things you say in anime; they're things you say when life gets real and you don't back down.

Tomorrow, we shift from battle mode to fan mode, learning how to compliment, admire, and express your fandom with real Japanese flair.

See you for fan expressions!

Scan to Listen

43%.....Complete!!

Day 14: Fan Expressions

Mission: Compliment Like a True Otaku

Sometimes, you just have to say it: That outfit? *Kawaii.* That character design? *Suki!* That cosplayer? *Kakkoii.* That new anime drop? *Subarashii.*

Today's mission is about learning how to admire out loud—to say what you like, love, or stan with confidence.

These aren't just words you hear at anime conventions; they're real Japanese compliments you'll hear in conversations, school hallways, even on Japanese Instagram. And when used right? They make you instantly more relatable, expressive, and connected.

Let's learn how to light someone up with a well-placed "*Kawaii!*" (or admit you're a fan with pride).

Phrases of the Day

Japanese	Pronunciation	Meaning
かわいい	*ka-waii*	Cute / Adorable
かっこいい	*ka-kkoii*	Cool / Stylish
すき	*su-ki*	I like you / I like it
おたく	*o-ta-ku*	Fan / Geek (original meaning)

How to Use Them

- ***かわいい (ka-waii)***: Japan's most iconic word. Say it when you see something cute—clothes, animals, art, people. Use a soft voice or a big gasp for effect. (*KAWAIII!*)

- **かっこいい *(ka-kkoii)***: Used to describe someone or something as cool, handsome, or stylish. Think: a fighter pose, slick outfit, or sleek car.
- **すき *(su-ki)***: A gentle way to say "I like" something—or someone. Context matters. It can mean "I love this anime" or "I'm low-key confessing feelings."
- **おたく *(o-ta-ku)***: Originally meant someone obsessed with a hobby. Once a mild insult, it's now reclaimed by proud fans. You can say "アニメおたく" (anime otaku) or "鉄道おたく" (train geek). Use with confidence and community love.

Try this: Say "*Kawaii!*" as if you saw the cutest plush ever. Now try "*Kakkoii!*" like someone just nailed a perfect pose.

Kanji of the Day: 愛

- **Meaning:** Love / Affection
- **Reading:** あい (*ai*)
- **Mnemonic:** A heart protected by hands—real love is something you hold carefully.

Seen in:

- 愛してる (*ai-shi-te-ru*) – I love you
- 愛情 (*ai-jou*) – deep affection
- 恋愛 (*ren'ai*) – romantic love

Stroke Order

It's a complex one, but beautiful. Think of it as building layers of feeling:

1. Top strokes = cover/protection
2. Middle = heart
3. Bottom = motion/action

Try tracing the kanji with your finger in the air while saying "*ai.*" This one's about emotion more than precision today.

Mini-Dialogue: Sharing a Compliment

A: そのコスプレ、かわいい！（*So-no ko-su-pu-re, ka-waii!* – That cosplay is so cute!)

B: ありがとう！あなたも、かっこいい！（*A-ri-ga-tou! A-na-ta mo, ka-kkoii!* – Thanks! You're cool too!)

A: このキャラ、すき〜（*Ko-no kya-ra, su-ki~* – I love this character!)

B: わかる！わたし、おたくだから。（*Wa-ka-ru!* – I feel you!)

See how it flows? These phrases bounce naturally at events, online, or just between fans who "get it."

Cultural Insight: From Shyness to Shininess

Japanese culture often avoids direct confrontation, but when it comes to admiration, people love to express aesthetic joy.

You'll hear "かわいい〜!" (*ka-waii!*) shouted in boutiques, whispered between friends, and screamed in reaction videos. The emotional honesty of words like "すき" (*su-ki*) or "かっこいい" (*ka-kkoii*) balances Japan's more reserved side.

- **Anime Moment:** In *K-On!*, every compliment is wrapped in friendship. In *Horimiya,* a whispered "すき" (*su-ki*) changes everything. In Love Live, "かわいい" (*ka-kkoii*) is the entire brand.
- **Fan Tip:** Use these phrases generously at fan events, artist tables, or on social media. Just add "です" (*de-su*) for a polite touch. Your energy will be welcomed.

Quick Quiz – 1 Minute

1. What does "すき" mean?
   a. Hate
   b. I like you / it
   c. Sorry
2. What's the meaning of "おたく"?
   a. Stranger
   b. Nerd / Fan
   c. Fighter
3. Which kanji means "love"?
   a. 心
   b. 気
   c. 愛

Bonus Challenge: Go on social media or look at something you love, then say: "すき!" (*su-ki*) or "かわいい!" (*ka-waii!*). Say it out loud. Make it real.

Answers: 1–b, 2–b, 3–c

XP Earned: 20

You just mastered *fandom fluency*. Say it with love!

Badge Progress: Anime Aficionado – 4/5 Days Complete. One more mission and you'll level up with your Anime Aficionado badge!

Final Thoughts

Today, you learned how to express admiration with clarity, joy, and heart.

These are connections. Even if you're telling someone they're cool, these are the phrases that build bridges in both language and love.

Tomorrow, we celebrate your fandom, your fluency, and your fun.

Let's bring it all together on Day 15!

Scan to Listen

46%.....Complete!!

Day 15: Finding Your Voice in Japanese

15

Mission: Don't Just Speak Japanese—Be Yourself in It

You just didn't learn how to say "cute" or "I like it" this week. You learned how to feel something and say it out loud.

That's a turning point in every language learner's journey: When it stops being about "getting it right" and starts being about "being real."

This day is about asking: "Who am I in Japanese?"

Your Japanese Persona

Language shapes personality. In Japanese, maybe you're…

- A little more soft-spoken.
- A total hype machine.
- Tender and honest.

That's the beautiful thing—you get to decide.

Reflection Prompt: Who are you when you speak Japanese? Are you playful? Shy? Bold? Encouraging?

Write 3 words that describe your Japanese self. Now pick your top signature phrase from this week—the one that feels most like you.

Expression Power-Up: Feeling Through Phrases

Let's turn words into identity. Here are a few personality phrases you now own:

- *がんばれ！* ***(gan-ba-re!)*** – You're the motivator.

- すき。***(su-ki)*** – You speak with your heart.
- しんけんだ！***(shin ken-da!)*** – You take things seriously.
- かわいい！***(ka-waii!)*** – You light up with joy.
- まけない！***(ma-ke-nai!)*** – You never back down.

Choose 2-3 and turn them into a short self-intro monologue. Like this:

よ！ がんばれって言うタイプ。しんけんだけど、アニメはぜったいにすき！（*Yo! Gan-ba-re tte iu tai-pu. Shin ken da-ke-do, a-ni-me wa ze-ttai ni su-ki!* / Yo! I'm the type to say "*ganbare.*" I'm serious—but I absolutely love anime!)

That's your Japanese voice. Keep shaping it.

Cultural Insight: The Language of Feeling Safe

In Japan, people don't always say exactly how they feel, but they create space for emotion with small words that open the door.

Words like:

- だいじょうぶ？（*Dai-jou-bu?* / Are you okay?)
- うれしい（*U-re-shii* / I'm happy)
- かなしい（*Ka-na-shii* / I'm sad)
- すき（*Su-ki* / I like you)

Using them takes emotional strength. Speaking them gives others permission to do the same.

This week, you learned how to create emotional safety in another language. That's a rare and powerful skill.

Final Challenge: Write Your Character Card

Like an anime bio or game profile—create your Japanese-speaking persona.

Include:

- A name or nickname.
- 3 traits.
- Your favorite phrase.
- Your emotional "special move" (like "がんばれ (*gab-ba-re*) beam!").
- A line you'd say at your most confident.

Example:

Name: ゆき (*Yu-ki*)

Traits: Friendly, emotional, bold.

Phrase: すき！(*Su-ki!*).

Special Move: "しんけんキック" (*shin ken ki-kku*) – when I'm serious, I go all in.

Line: よ！アニメのことなら、ぜったいにまけない！(*Yo! A-ni-me no ko-to-na-ra, ze-ttai-ni ma-ke-nai!* / Yo! When it comes to anime, I will never give up!)

You've gone from saying words to living in them.

Quiz – Know Your Voice

1. What's the difference between "すき" and "だいすき"？
   a. すき = like, だいすき = really like
   b. They mean the same
   c. だいすき is only used in anime
2. Which phrase could cheer someone up?

a. だめ
b. がんばれ
c. かなしい

3. Which kanji means "heart"?

a. 心
b. 気
c. 力

Answers: 1- a, 2- b, 3-a

XP Earned: 20

You finished Week 3! You've leveled up your emotional voice.

Badge Earned: Anime Aficionado

You now speak the language of fandom with clarity, confidence, and joy.

Week 3: Gem of Expression

This week, something shifted.

Through anime moments, emotional words, and daily mini-dialogues, you brought your inner voice to life.

That's what this gem is about: being seen, heard, and felt—even across languages.

Gem of Expression Earned

Language isn't just learned; it's lived.

Final Thoughts

You didn't just survive another week. You opened up. You connected. You expressed joy, love, and emotion in a new language.

This week, Japanese became more than vocabulary. It became a voice you can trust.

Next week? We go social. You'll learn how to make friends, compliment others, keep small talk going, and build real-life connections.

See you for Week 4! Let's make some friends in Japanese.

Scan to Listen

50%.....Complete!!

Personal Phrase Journal

Week 3: Anime and Pop Culture

Focus: Saying how you feel, anime influence, speaking from the heart.

A Phrase That Felt Personal

Japanese: ____________________

Romaji: ____________________

English: ____________________

Why did it resonate?

____

____

My "Anime Energy" Phrase of the Week

Phrase: ____________________

Which anime character might say this?

____

Words That Match My Mood

1. ____________________
2. ____________________
3. ____________________

Next Week's Intention

- ❑ Use an expressive phrase in real life
- ❑ Say something kind in Japanese
- ❑ Speak confidently even if I mess up

A QUICK FAVOR

How's your quest going, fellow adventurer?

If you're enjoying this book and finding it helpful, would you mind taking 2 minutes to leave a quick review on Amazon?

Your review helps other Japanese learners discover this book and know what to expect.

Even something simple like "Clear and easy to follow" or "Great daily structure" makes a huge difference for other beginners.

Scan to Leave a Review

The optimal approach? Share a short video where you discuss your thoughts on the book! If that feels like too much, there's absolutely no pressure. Providing feedback along with a couple of photos of the book would still be greatly appreciated!

Note: There's no obligation whatsoever, but it would be immensely valued!

Thank you for helping other learners!

Now, let's get back to your Japanese quest...

Week 4: Social Situations

Speak to Connect, Not Just to Communicate

You've ordered food, gone to a train station, shouted anime catchphrases with confidence, and now it's time to bring that language into real relationships.

This week, we step into the heart of connection:

- Introducing yourself
- Giving genuine compliments
- Making small talk
- Inviting someone to hang out
- Building trust with your words, tone, and energy

Because language isn't just a tool; it's a bridge. And this week, you'll learn how to cross it.

You'll learn how to start and sustain conversations that matter, even if you're meeting someone at a convention, in a classroom, or just hanging out with new friends online or abroad.

No stiff phrases. No robotic scripts. Just real-life Japanese for real human moments.

What You'll Learn This Week

This week, you'll learn:

- How to introduce yourself in a natural, friendly way.
- How to ask someone's name (without awkwardness).
- How to give compliments—both playful and sincere.
- How to talk about hobbies, interests, and how you're feeling.
- How to extend invitations and respond to them.
- Kanji that are connected to people, actions, and beauty.
- Social phrases you'll hear in anime and real life.

Why This Week Matters

Up until now, you've been gathering tools. This week, you'll learn how to use them to build connection.

Speaking with someone new in a different language can feel intimidating, but when you can say, "Hi, I'm [Your Name]" or "You're really good at that," suddenly… a door opens.

This is how you go from traveler to friend. From learner to participant.

You'll learn to ask questions. Express admiration. Talk about your day. And when you do? People lean in. They listen. They respond.

You don't need 500 vocabulary words to connect. You need just a few phrases and the confidence to use them.

This week will show you exactly how.

That's what I'm here for.

This week is where everything clicks.

You're no longer just learning how to say things; you're learning how to say you. To speak from your heart. To make a stranger smile. To say, "Let's be friends" with words and warmth.

And that starts tomorrow with something simple, but powerful: introducing yourself with confidence.

Let's go to Day 16! Your future friendships are waiting.

Day 16: Make Introductions

16

Mission: Say Who You Are (and Mean It)

There's something powerful about being able to walk up to someone, look them in the eye, and say: "Hi. My name is…" It's a tiny sentence, but it opens big doors.

Today, we're learning how to introduce ourselves in Japanese, ask someone their name, and say "friend"—the word that turns strangers into something more.

These phrases are simple, honest, and filled with possibility.

Even if you're at a Japanese class, anime convention, or just meeting someone online, you'll know exactly what to say.

Phrases of the Day

Japanese	Pronunciation	Meaning
なまえは?	*na-mae wa?*	What's your name?
わたしは [Name]	*wa-ta-shi wa [Name]*	I'm [Name]
ともだち	*to-mo-da-chi*	Friend
たのしい	*ta-no-shii*	Fun / Enjoyable

How to Use Them

- ***なまえは? (na-mae wa?)***: Friendly and casual way to ask, "What's your name?" You can also say "おなまえは?" to be politer.
- ***わたしは* [Name] *(wa-ta-shi wa [name])***: Say this to share your name: "わたしは エミです" = "I'm Emi." Bonus: If you're feeling confident, add "よろしく" (*yo-ro-shi-ku*) afterward, which means "Nice to meet you."

- ***ともだち(to-mo-da-chi)***: The sweetest word. "Friend." Use it to describe someone you like or to ask someone to be your friend: "ともだち?" = "Friends?"
- ***たのしい (ta-no-shii)***: Use this to describe something as fun: a class, a game, a day, a person. Say it with a smile—it's a feeling, not just a word.

Try this: Say "わたしは [your name]" clearly. Then ask yourself, "なまえは?" in the mirror like you're meeting someone new.

Kanji of the Day: 名

- **Meaning:** Name
- **Reading:** な (*na*), めい (*mei*)
- **Mnemonic:** Imagine a "mouth speaking in the evening" to give someone a name.

You'll see it in:

- 名前 (*na-mae*) – name
- 有名 (*yuu-mei*) – famous
- 名刺 (*mei-shi*) – name card (business card)

Stroke Order

1. Top horizontal
2. Vertical through
3. Evening radical on bottom

Try writing 名 once while saying "*na.*" Draw your name tag next to it!

Mini-Dialogue: Making a New Friend

A: なまえは? (*Na-mae wa?* – What's your name?)

B: わたしは ミカです。あなたは? (*Wa-ta-shi wa Mi-ka desu. A-na-ta wa?* – I'm Mika. And you?)

A: わたしは ジュン。ともだち? (*Wa-ta-shi wa Jun. To-mo-da-chi?* – I'm Jun. Friends?)

B: うん!たのしいね! (*Un! Ta-no-shii ne!* – Yeah! This is fun!)

This dialogue is sweet, light, and 100% realistic. Use it any time you meet someone new.

Cultural Insight: How Japanese People Introduce Themselves

In Japan, introductions often follow a slightly formal structure, even among peers:

"はじめまして。わたしは [Name] です。よろしくおねがいします。" (*Ha-ji-me-ma-shi-te. Wa-ta-shi wa* [name]*de-su. Yo-ro-shi-ku o-ne-gai shi-ma-su* / Nice to meet you. I'm [Name]. Please be kind to me.)

It may sound formal in English, but in Japanese, it's warm and respectful. In casual settings (like anime clubs or meetups), people skip the long version and simply say: "[Name] です。よろしく～!" ([Name]*de-su. Yo-ro-shi-ku ~!*)

- **Anime Moment:** In *Shirobako,* new team members introduce themselves with humble smiles. In *My Hero Academia,* every student introduces themselves before training. And in *Fruits Basket,* friendships blossom from a single "ともだち?" (*To-mo-da-chi?*).
- **Travel Tip:** In Japan, exchanging names is often done with a small bow and maybe a business card if it's formal. But a friendly "わたしは ___ です" (*Wa-ta-shi wa* [name] *de-su*) and a warm smile go a long way—even if you're at a cat café or language exchange.

Quick Quiz – 1 Minute

1. What does "なまえは?" mean?
    a. Where are you from?
    b. What's your name?
    c. How old are you?
2. What's the meaning of "ともだち" ?
    a. Teacher
    b. Stranger
    c. Friend
3. Which kanji means "name"?
    a. 名
    b. 心
    c. 日

Bonus Prompt: Fill in this sentence: "わたしは ________。ともだち?" (*Wa-ta-shi wa ________. To-mo-da-chi?*). Try it with your real name!

Answers: 1–b, 2–c, 3–a

XP Earned: 20

You just introduced yourself... in Japanese. That's a huge step forward.

Badge Progress: Social Star – 1/5 Days Complete. You're no longer just learning; you're connecting.

Final Thoughts

This was about opening up. The moment you say "わたしは…" (*wa-ta-shi wa*) in a new language, you're not just speaking; you're arriving.

You're now equipped to meet someone new, ask their name, and make them feel welcome. That's not beginner energy. That's community energy.

Tomorrow, we learn how to make someone's day with a well-placed compliment.

See you for Day 17!

Scan to Listen

53%.....Complete!!

Day 17: Give Compliments

17

Mission: Make Someone Smile (in Japanese)

Compliments are simple but powerful.

A kind word can brighten someone's day, build a friendship, or open a door to deeper conversation. And in Japanese, compliments carry a unique charm; they're often gentle, sincere, and slightly humble.

Today's mission is to learn how to give compliments in ways that feel authentic, respectful, and fun.

Whether you're admiring someone's outfit, their skills, or their kindness, these words will help you express it with warmth and confidence.

Let's learn how to say, "You're amazing"—and mean it.

Phrases of the Day

Japanese	Pronunciation	Meaning
じょうず	*jou-zu*	Skilled / Good at it
きれい	*ki-rei*	Pretty / Beautiful / Clean
すてき	*su-te-ki*	Lovely / Wonderful
すばらしい	*su-ba-ra-shii*	Amazing / Superb

How to Use Them

- **じょうず *(jou-zu)***: Use this when someone does something well, like drawing, singing, cooking, or even speaking Japanese! "日本語、じょうず！" = "Your Japanese is great!"
- **きれい *(ki-rei)***: Means "pretty," "beautiful," or "neat." Use it for people, places, handwriting, or even a view. "きれいな 花" = "A beautiful flower."

- すてき ***(su-te-ki)***: A stylish, slightly elegant word that means "lovely," "wonderful," or even "charming." Compliment someone's vibe with this!
- すばらしい ***(su-ba-ra-shii)***: A dramatic "amazing!"—you'll hear it in anime a lot. Great for big praise: a powerful performance, a moving story, an epic cosplay.

Practice Tip: Say "すばらしい!" with a dramatic anime voice. Then whisper "すてき…" like you're admiring a sunset or a beautiful outfit.

Kanji of the Day: 美

- **Meaning:** Beauty
- **Reading:** び (*bai*)
- **Mnemonic:** A person with long flowing hair—a classic image of beauty in ancient art.

Seen in:

- 美しい (*ut-su-ku-shii*) – beautiful.
- 美人 (*bai-jin*) – beautiful person.
- 美術 (*bai-jut-su*) – fine art.
- 美学 (*bai-ga-ku*) – aesthetics.

Stroke Order

1. Top radical = "sheep" (a symbol of beauty)
2. Bottom strokes = "big" (like large presence or impact)

Trace it slowly while saying "*bai... bai...*" like you're admiring something you love.

Mini-Dialogue: Giving a Compliment

A: わあ、そのえ、きれい！（*Waa, so-no e, ki-rei!* – Wow, that picture is beautiful!）

B: ありがとう～（*A-ri-ga-tou~* – Thank you~）

A: ほんとに、じょうず。すばらしい！（*Hon-to ni, jou-zu. Su-ba-ra-shii!* – Really, you're skilled. Amazing!）

B: えへへ、うれしい！（*Ehehe, u-re-shii!* – Aww, I'm happy!）

Compliments + emotion = connection. Keep it light, sincere, and let your face do half the work.

Cultural Insight: Compliments With Humility

In Japan, people often deflect compliments modestly. You'll often hear:

- "そんなことないです～"（*So-nna ko-to nai-de-su ~* / It's not that great…）
- "まだまだです。"（*Ma-da-ma-da-de-su* / I still have a long way to go.）

It's not rejection; it's just humility. Don't worry! Your compliment still means the world. Just smile and follow up with "でも、ほんとに すてき！"（*De-mo, hon-to-ni su-te-ki!* / But really, it's lovely!）

- **Anime Moment:** In *Kaguya-Sama: Love Is War,* even compliments turn into battles. In *Your Name,* the softest "きれい…"（*ki-rei…*）carries so much emotion. And in *Violet Evergarden,* "すばらしい"（*su-ba-ra-shii*）becomes a way to express awe and grief all at once.
- **Travel Tip:** Compliment cosplayers with "すごい！"（*su-goi!*）or "すてき！"（*su-te-ki!*）to show genuine appreciation. You'll often get a grateful (and bashful) "ありがとう～"（*a-ri-ga-tou*）in return.

Quick Quiz – 1 Minute

1. What does "じょうず" mean?
    a. Beautiful
    b. Skilled
    c. Quiet
2. Which phrase means "amazing"?
    a. すばらしい
    b. たのしい
    c. だいじょうぶ
3. Which kanji means "beauty"?
    a. 名
    b. 愛 c
    c. 美

Bonus Prompt: Think of someone you admire (real or fictional) and say: "[Name] は、すてき!" ([Name] *wa, su-te-ki!*) Say it like you're really in awe. That's when language sticks.

Answers: 1–b, 2–a, 3–c

XP Earned: 20

You just gave your first *Japanese compliments.* That's social power!

Badge Progress: Social Star – 2/5 Days Complete. You're no longer just talking; you're uplifting.

Final Thoughts

Compliments don't have to be perfect. They just have to be true. With today's phrases, you can speak appreciation into the world, and that changes everything.

So next time you see something beautiful, talented, or simply kind, try saying it in Japanese.

Tomorrow, we make things even more natural··· by learning how to chit-chat.

See you for Day 18!

Scan to Listen

56%.....Complete!!

Day 18: Small Talk

18

Mission: Break the Ice With Ease

Big conversations don't always start with big words. Sometimes they start with: "Nice weather, huh?" "What do you like to do?" "Do you like Japan?"

Small talk might seem, well, small··· but in Japanese (and real life), it's a powerful way to build connection.

Today's mission is to learn how to chit-chat casually—the kind of light conversation that turns into laughter, friendship, and maybe even love, anime-style.

Let's make talking feel easy.

Phrases of the Day

Japanese	Pronunciation	Meaning
おげんき?	*o-gen-ki?*	How are you?
しゅみは?	*shu-mi wa?*	What's your hobby?
にほんすき?	*ni-hon su-ki?*	Do you like Japan?
てんきいい	*ten-ki ii*	The weather's nice

How to Use Them

- **おげんき?*(o-gen-ki)***: This is a polite, caring way to ask "How are you?" Use it with friends or people you haven't seen in a while.
- **しゅみは? *(shu-mi wa?)***: Literally, "Hobby?"—a casual way to ask, "What do you like to do?" It's a great starter question for any age group.

- にほんすき？ ***(ni-hon su-ki?)***: "Do you like Japan?"—Perfect for fellow anime lovers, travelers, or when someone asks why you're learning Japanese.
- てんきいい ***(ten-ki ii)***: Simple weather opener: "The weather's nice." It can be used to break the silence or start a light conversation.

Try this: Say "しゅみは？" (*shu-mi-wa?*) like you're curious and relaxed. Then try "おげんき？" (*o-gen-ki?*) with a warm, checking-in tone.

Kanji of the Day: 日

- **Meaning:** Day / Sun
- **Reading:** にち (*ni-chi*), ひ (*hi*)
- **Mnemonic:** Looks like a window with sunlight shining through—symbolizing time and brightness.

You'll see it in:

- 今日 (*kyou*) – today
- 日曜日 (*ni-chi-you-bi*) – Sunday
- 日本 (*ni-hon*) – Japan
- 毎日 (*mai-ni-chi*) – every day

Stroke Order

1. Top horizontal
2. Vertical through
3. Close the square
4. Middle line = the sunbeam

Write it once while saying "*hi*" or "*nichi*"—a little light in your practice.

Mini-Dialogue: Sweet, Casual Talk

A: おげんき? (*O-gen-ki?* – How are you?)

B: うん、げんき。しゅみは? (*Un, gen-ki. Shu-mi wa?* – Yeah, I'm good. What's your hobby?)

A: アニメ!にほんすき～ (*A-ni-me! Ni-hon su-ki~* – Anime! I love Japan~)

B: わかる! てんきいいね、きょう。(*Wa-ka-ru! Ten-ki ii ne, kyou.* – I know, right? The weather's nice today.)

You just had a whole slice-of-life anime moment. All in under 30 seconds.

Cultural Insight: The Art of Light Conversation

In Japanese culture, small talk often stays light and kind, especially early on in relationships. Topics like weather, hobbies, favorite foods, and weekend plans are safe and friendly.

Sometimes, just saying "てんきいいね" (*ten-ki ii ne*) while sitting next to someone is enough to open the door.

- **Anime Moment:** In *Fruits Basket,* small talk turns into healing. In *Yuru Camp,* weather and food are the conversation. In *Your Name,* casual questions become deep moments of connection.
- **Travel Tip:** Want to connect with Japanese people online or in person? Start with: "こんにちは!おげんき?" (*ko-ni-chi-wa, o gen-ki?*). It's simple. It's sweet. And it works.

Quick Quiz – 1 Minute

1. What does "しゅみは?" mean?

    a. What's your name?

b. What's your hobby?

c. Where are you from?

2. What's the meaning of "てんきいい" ?

a. Let's hang out

b. Nice to meet you

c. The weather's nice

3. Which kanji means "day" or "sun"?

a. 名

b. 日

c. 美

Bonus Prompt: Try writing this sentence in romaji (Japanese written using our letters): "*Anime suki? Shumi wa?*" Say it to yourself—or better yet, a fellow fan!

Answers: 1–b, 2–c, 3–b

XP Earned: 20

You now speak the *language of connection.*

Badge Progress: Social Star – 3/5 Days Complete. You're halfway to mastering everyday friendships.

Final Thoughts

Today wasn't just about learning what to say; it was about how to relate. Small talk is the first step to big trust, big laughter, and big friendship.

You now know how to ask someone how they are, what they enjoy, and how they're experiencing the day.

Tomorrow, we go one step further: inviting someone to join you.

See you for Day 19! Let's keep building beautiful connections.

Scan to Listen

60%.....Complete!!

Day 19: Extend Invitations

19

Mission: Ask Someone to Join You

Sometimes the hardest part isn't saying hello; it's saying "Wanna come with me?"

Today's mission is all about inviting people into your world to hang out, join an activity, or go on a little adventure. Even if it's coffee, karaoke, a convention, or a casual stroll under cherry blossoms, these phrases give you the tools to ask with clarity and warmth.

They're also the key to making someone feel welcome, included, and appreciated. Let's learn how to say "Come with me?"—in Japanese.

Phrases of the Day

Japanese	Pronunciation	Meaning
きてください	*ki-te ku-da-sai*	Please come
あそびましょう	*a-so-bi-ma-shou*	Let's hang out / play together
いつ?	*it-su?*	When?
いいね!	*ii ne!*	Sounds good! / Nice!

How to Use Them

- **きてください *(ki-te ku-da-sai)***: A polite but warm way to invite someone—literally "please come." Use it when inviting someone to an event, your house, or a gathering.
- **あそびましょう *(a-so-bi-ma-shou)***: "Let's hang out!" or "Let's play!" It's cheerful, friendly, and super common in anime and real life. Use it with classmates, coworkers, or new friends.

- いつ? ***(it-su?)***: Just one word: "When?" It's a great way to keep the invite going or to respond when someone else suggests plans.
- いいね! ***(ii ne!)***: A sweet, casual "Sounds great!" Use it to show enthusiasm or agree to someone's suggestion.

Try this: Say "あそびましょう!" (*A-so-bi-ma-shou!*) like you're inviting someone to do something fun.

Kanji of the Day: 行

- **Meaning:** Go / Move / Travel
- **Reading:** い (*i*), こう (*kou*), おこな (*o-ko-nau*)
- **Mnemonic:** Picture a path or crossroads—this is the kanji for action, for going places, for moving forward.

Seen in:

- 行く (*i-ku*) – to go.
- 銀行 (*gin-kou*) – bank.
- 旅行 (*ryo-kou*) – travel.
- 行動 (*kou-dou*) – action.

Stroke Order

1. Horizontal top line
2. Vertical through the center
3. Left and right "legs" of the journey

Write 行 once and say "*iku... iku...*"—you're moving forward!

Mini-Dialogue: Making Plans

A: あそびましょう！(*A-so-bi-ma-shou!* – Let's hang out!)

B: いいね！ いつ？(*Ii ne! It-su?* – Sounds great! When?)

A: あした、きてください！(*A-shi-ta, ki-te ku-da-sai!* – Come tomorrow!)

B: はい、いくよ！(*Hai, i-ku yo!* – Okay, I'll go!)

These are phrases you'll hear all the time in slice-of-life anime, youth dramas, or daily school life in Japan. Now they're yours to use.

Cultural Insight: Inviting With Warmth

In Japanese culture, invitations are often wrapped in kindness and suggestion rather than pressure. That's why phrases like "～ましょう" (Let's…) feel so light and welcoming.

There's also a high cultural value placed on not making others feel obligated, so these invitation phrases help you sound thoughtful and friendly, without overstepping.

- **Anime Moment:** In *Horimiya,* characters use soft invitations like "いっしょに行こうか？" (*I-ssho ni i-kou ka?* / Shall we go together?) to express closeness. In *Yuru Camp,* a gentle "あそびましょう" (*a-so-bi-ma-shou* / Let's play) turns into full-on friendship over hot cocoa and campfires.
- **Travel Tip:** If you're planning to meet Japanese friends or penpals, phrases like "きてください" (*ki-te ku-da-sai!*) and "いいね！" (*ii-ne!*) are polite and fun. Don't be afraid to initiate!

Quick Quiz – 1 Minute

1. What does "あそびましょう" mean?
   a. Let's hang out
   b. What are you doing?
   c. Come here
2. What's the meaning of "いいね"？
   a. I'm busy
   b. Let's go
   c. Sounds good!
3. Which kanji means "go"?
   a. 行
   b. 名
   c. 力

Bonus Prompt: Invite someone (real or imaginary) to hang out in Japanese: "あそびましょう！ いつ？" (*A-so-bi-ma-shou! It-su?*) Say it out loud, like you mean it.

XP Earned: 20

You now know how to say "Come with me" in Japanese.

Badge Progress: Social Star – 4/5 Days Complete. One more day and you'll earn your badge in connection and kindness.

Final Thoughts

Inviting someone is a gift, and now you can do it in Japanese. Even if it's a casual hangout, a cultural event, or just watching anime together, these words let people know: I want you there.

And that? That's language with heart.

Tomorrow, we close out this beautiful week with a celebration of your growth and connection.

See you for Day 20!

Scan to Listen

63%.....Complete!!

Day 20: Your Japanese Is a Bridge 20

Mission: Reflect on How Far You've Come—And How It's Changing You

You came into this journey with curiosity. Now you're walking out of Week 4 with connection.

Not just words, but warmth. Not just grammar, but genuine interaction.

This week, you asked someone's name. You gave compliments. You invited someone to hang out. And maybe··· you saw a new side of yourself while doing it.

So today's not about what you "should" say in Japanese. It's about what you want to say. Who you want to be. What kind of presence you want to bring into the room—any room—when speaking this language.

Reflection Prompt: Language as Self-Expression

Answer these out loud—or write them down:

- What surprised you most about talking with someone in Japanese?
- How did it feel to say your name, compliment someone, or suggest hanging out?
- What kind of energy do you bring when you speak Japanese? Playful? Gentle? Brave?

Now finish this sentence:

When I speak Japanese, I feel ___________.

That's identity.

Connection Challenge: Your Japanese Introduction

Let's build your own short intro—the one you'd give at a meetup, language exchange, or anime convention.

Use this as a flexible script to build from:

はじめまして!わたしは [your name] です。アニメが すきです。しゅみは [your hobby]。ともだち、ほしいです!あそびましょう? (*Ha-ji-me-ma-shi-te! Wa-ta-shi wa* [your name]*de-su. A-ni-me ga su-ki-de-su. Shi ~yu-mi-ha* [your hobby]. *To-mo-da-chi, ho-shii-de-su! A-so-bi-ma-shou?*)

Now: Say it. Really say it. Smile when you do. You're putting your voice into the world—and that's no small thing.

Cultural Reflection: Belonging in a New Language

In Japan, politeness isn't just a rule; it's a welcome mat. Every ありがとう (*a-ri-ga-tou*) and すてき (*su-te-ki*) carries weight.

Even as a beginner, your effort builds bridges. When you ask "おげんき?" (*o gen-ki*) or say "いいね!" (*ii-ne!*) with joy, you're offering more than a phrase. You're saying:

"I want to meet you where you are." "I'm learning this for you." "Let's connect."

That's real. That's rare. That's beautiful.

Anime Moment: From Stranger to Friend

In anime, entire friendships blossom from one compliment or hobby chat:

- In *Fruits Basket,* Tohru's kind words turn a broken boy into a friend.

- In *K-On!*, "Let's hang out" becomes "Let's play music together."
- In *Horimiya*, one simple conversation unlocks two hidden worlds.

You've now got the language to start your own version of that story.

Final Challenge: Send a Real or Imagined Text

Write a casual message to someone in Japanese using this week's phrases.

Example: なまえは?わたしは ひろ!アニメ、すき?あそびましょう!いつ? (*Na-mae wa? Wa-ta-shi wa Hi-ro! A-ni-me, su-ki? A-so-bi-ma-shou! It-su?*)

Whether it's real or practice, you're speaking with intention now.

XP Earned: 20

You completed Week 4! You've mastered introductions, compliments, casual convo, and kind invitations.

Badge Earned: Social Star

You now speak Japanese with kindness, connection, and community energy.

Week 4: Gem of Confidence

Confidence doesn't come from knowing it all; it comes from showing up again and again.

This week, you learned how to handle social life in Japanese: asking for things, showing appreciation. You've practiced enough to speak without freezing.

That's what this gem honors: the boldness to speak even when you're still learning.

Gem of Confidence Earned

You don't need perfection. You've got presence. Keep going.

Final Thoughts

You're not learning Japanese anymore. You're using it to connect with others, with culture, with your own sense of self.

This week, you became more than a language learner. You became someone who can make others feel welcome.

That's fluency. That's power. That's you.

Next up, you'll learn to handle sticky situations, offer help, stay calm, and express thanks when it matters most.

Let's take this voice of yours—and turn it into something unshakable.

Scan to Listen

66%.....Complete!!

Personal Phrase Journal

Week 4: Social Situations

Focus: Friendship, small talk, compliments, making connections.

A Time I Imagined Making a Friend in Japanese

What would I say?

____

How would they reply?

____

Phrases That Make Me Sound Friendly

1. ______________________________
2. ______________________________
3. ______________________________

A Compliment I Loved Learning

Phrase: ______________________________

Why did it feel good?

____

____

____

Next Week's Intention

- ❏ Initiate small talk
- ❏ Compliment someone
- ❏ Text a language partner
- ❏ Other: ______________________________

Week 5: Practical Scenarios

Stay Calm. Speak Clearly. Be Ready.

Real fluency isn't just about cute phrases and friendly conversations. It's about being able to ask for help when something's wrong. To say you're sorry. To say "I'm okay." To thank someone who showed you kindness.

This week is different. It's real-life readiness.

Because sometimes, Japanese fluency doesn't sound flashy; it sounds kind, clear, and composed.

What You'll Learn This Week

This week, you'll learn:

- Essential phrases for asking for help or assistance.
- Emergency vocabulary (hospital, police, okay/not okay).
- How to apologize gracefully and express regret.
- Useful questions when you don't understand something.
- How to show appreciation and gratitude.
- Kanji related to illness, apology, questioning, and emotion.

This isn't the dramatic part of the journey; this is the important part. These are the words that give you calm in chaos.

Why This Week Matters

Let's be honest: Life doesn't always go as planned. You might:

- Get lost in a busy train station.
- Feel unwell or confused.
- Accidentally bump into someone.
- Need help, directions, or clarification.
- Want to thank someone for going out of their way.

This week, you're getting prepared for those moments with emotional intelligence. No panic. No guessing. Just calm, respectful phrases that help you stay in control—and help others help you.

These are the words that don't just help you, they help others help you. They show you care. That you're listening. That you're growing.

That's the kind of language we practice this week: real, raw, respectful.

This week, you move from conversation to compassion. From small talk to real talk. From reacting with panic to responding with purpose.

This is where your Japanese becomes more than a skill; it becomes a lifeline.

And tomorrow, we begin with one of the most important things anyone can say:

"Help, please."

Let's go to Day 21!

Day 21: Ask for Help

Mission: Stay Calm, Speak Up, and Get Support

Sometimes, things go wrong. You feel sick. You get lost. Someone near you needs help... fast.

In these moments, your ability to say even one clear phrase can make all the difference.

Today's mission is simple but powerful: Learn how to ask for help in Japanese.

Because when you know how to speak up, you're helping yourself and giving others the chance to support you.

Let's build that strength together.

Phrases of the Day

Japanese	Pronunciation	Meaning
ほんとう?	*hon-tou?*	Really? / Are you sure?
びょういんはどこ?	*byou-in wa do-ko?*	Where's the hospital?
けいさつ	*kei-sat-su*	Police
だいじょうぶです	*dai-jou-bu de-su*	I'm okay / It's okay

How to Use Them

- ***ほんとう? (hon-tou?)***: A gentle way to ask, "Really?" It can be used when someone offers help or says everything's okay. It can mean "Are you sure?" or "Is it true?"
- ***びょういんはどこ? (byou-in wa do-ko?)***: "Where's the hospital?" This is one of the most useful phrases in an

emergency. You can also say it politely with "ですか" at the end: "びょういんはどこですか?"

- **けいさつ *(kei-sat-su)***: "Police." Use this word alone or with "よんでください" (please call): "けいさつを よんでください!" = "Please call the police!"
- **だいじょうぶです *(dai-jou-bu de-su)***: "I'm okay." This is a phrase of comfort and reassurance. You can use it to let others know you're fine—or to ask gently: "だいじょうぶ?" = "Are you okay?"

Practice Tip: Say "だいじょうぶです" (*dai-jou-bu de-su*) slowly and gently. Let it feel like a calming phrase. Then say "けいさつ" (*kei-sat-su*) firmly, like you mean it. Tone matters here.

Kanji of the Day: 病

- **Meaning:** Illness / Sickness
- **Reading:** びょう (*byou*)
- **Mnemonic:** Think of a person lying in bed under a roof—this kanji shows someone unwell and needs care.

Seen in:

- 病院 (*byou-in*) – hospital
- 病気 (*byou-ki*) – illness
- 急病 (*kyuu-byou*) – sudden illness

Stroke Order

1. Left radical = "sickness"
2. Right side = two strokes for shelter + person

Write it once and say "*byou.*" Imagine the care behind the kanji. This one means safety and support.

Mini-Dialogue: Asking for Help

A: ごめん… びょういんはどこ? (*Go-men... Byou-in wa do-ko?* – Excuse me… Where's the hospital?)

B: あそこです。だいじょうぶ? (*A-so-ko de-su. Dai-jou-bu?* – Over there. Are you okay?)

A: うん… ありがとう。ほんとうに。(*Un... A-ri-ga-tou. Hon-tou ni.* – Yeah… Thank you. Really.)

This isn't dramatic; it's grounded, kind, and real. Practice it like you're helping, not just reacting.

Cultural Insight: Help Comes Quietly

In Japan, people often hesitate to ask for help—they don't want to cause trouble (*mei-wa-ku*). But here's the truth: Asking calmly isn't trouble; it's clarity.

If you say "すみません" (*su-mi-ma-sen*) and clearly ask for help, most Japanese people will stop and try—whether with directions, assistance, or just presence.

- **Anime Moment:** In *Tokyo Revengers,* the word "たすけて" (*Ta-su-ke-te* / Help me) changes the course of the story. In *A Silent Voice,* asking for help brings healing. *In Erased,* quiet moments of concern— "だいじょうぶ?" (*dai-jou-bu?* / Are you okay?)—hold everything together.
- **Travel Tip:** If you feel sick, lost, or scared, say "びょういんはどこですか?" (*Byou in wa do-ko-de-su ka?* / Where's the hospital?) with your calmest voice. Pair it with body language, and help will find you.

Quick Quiz – 1 Minute

1. What does "けいさつ" mean?
    a. Ambulance
    b. Police
    c. Fire
2. How do you say "Where's the hospital?"
    a. びょういんはどこ?
    b. けいさつはどこ?
    c. おみせはどこ?
3. What's the meaning of "だいじょうぶです"？
    a. I'm lost
    b. I'm okay
    c. I don't know

Bonus Prompt: Say this out loud, slowly and calmly: "びょういんはどこですか?" (*Byou in wa do-ko-de-su ka?*). Even practicing it makes you more prepared. That's strength.

Answers: 1–b, 2–a, 3–b

XP Earned: 20

You now know how to ask for help—clearly and calmly. That's real fluency.

Badge Progress: Problem-Solver Pro – 1/5 Days Complete. You've started your journey toward grace under pressure.

Final Thoughts

Today, you didn't just learn a phrase; you learned how to stay steady. You can now say:

- "Where's the hospital?"
- "Please call the police."
- "I'm okay."
- "Really?"

In a hard moment, that's more than language. That's peace in action. Tomorrow, we change from help to healing, with the language of apology and grace.

See you for Day 22!

Scan to Listen

70%.....Complete!!

Day 22: Apologize Gracefully

22

Mission: Say "I'm Sorry" With Heart

In any language, apologizing isn't weakness, it's wisdom. It takes courage to say: "I was wrong." "That was rude." "I didn't mean to hurt you."

In Japanese, apologies are more than words. They're a gesture of respect. A bridge between people. A quiet reset.

Today, you'll learn how to say "I'm sorry" sincerely, softly, and in the right context—whether you bump into someone, run late, or just need to make peace.

Phrases of the Day

Japanese	Pronunciation	Meaning
ごめんなさい	*go-men na-sai*	I'm sorry
しつれい	*shi-tsu-rei*	Excuse me / I was rude
わるい	*wa-rui*	My bad / That was wrong

How to Use Them

- ***ごめんなさい (go-men na-sai)***: The go-to heartfelt apology. Say it when you hurt someone, accidentally offend, or need to admit fault. Soft tone = sincere tone.
- ***しつれい (shi-tsu-rei)***: Literally means "rudeness." Use this if you accidentally interrupt someone, speak out of turn, or bump into them in a formal setting. Also works as a polite "Excuse me."
- ***わるい (wa-rui)***: Super casual "my bad." Use with close friends or when teasingly admitting something small. Like: "*Ah, warui~*"

Try this: Say “ごめんなさい” (*go-me-na-sai*) in a soft, steady voice. Now try “しつれいしました” (*Shi-tsu rei shi-ma-shi-ta*) with a small bow. This is presence in apology.

Kanji of the Day: 謝

- **Meaning:** Apologize
- **Reading:** しゃ (*sha*), あやま (*a-ya-ma*)
- **Mnemonic:** Words that bow—the kanji has the “word” radical and a complex symbol that represents humble intention.

Seen in:

- 謝る (*a-ya-ma-ru*) – to apologize
- 感謝 (*kan-sha*) – gratitude (literally “feel + apologize”)
- 謝罪 (*sha-zai*) – formal apology

Stroke Order

1. Left radical = “say”
2. Right side = flowing strokes for thought/action

Write it once and say “*sha.*” Bow your head as you finish—it builds muscle memory with respect.

Mini-Dialogue: Graceful Apology

A: ごめんなさい！(*Go-men na-sai!* – I’m so sorry!)

B: だいじょうぶ。きにしないで。(*Dai-jou-bu. Ki-ni shi-nai-de.* – It’s okay. Don’t worry about it.)

A: しつれいしました。(*Shi-tsu-rei shi-ma-shi-ta.* – Excuse me / I was rude.)

B: わたしも わるかった。(*Wa-ta-shi mo wa-ru-ka-tta.* – I was also in the wrong.)

That? That's reconciliation. These are the phrases that restore connection.

Cultural Insight: The Power of a Bow

In Japan, apologies often come with a bow. The deeper the bow, the deeper the regret. But even a small nod adds weight to the words.

Japanese culture values accountability without confrontation. Saying "ごめんなさい" (*go-me-na-sai*) isn't dramatic; it's mature. It clears the air and opens the door.

- **Anime Moment:** In *Jujutsu Kaisen,* Yuji bows deeply after failing to save someone. In *Violet Evergarden,* every letter is an apology or thank-you wrapped in beauty. In *March Comes in Like a Lion,* "しつれいしました" (*Shi-tsu rei shi-ma-shita* / Sorry for the inconvenience) becomes a turning point of healing.
- **Travel Tip:** If you bump into someone, say "ごめんなさい" (*go-me-na-sai*) softly with a small bow. It's always appreciated and sometimes met with a smile.

Quick Quiz – 1 Minute

1. What does "しつれい" mean?

   a. Trouble

   b. Excuse me / I was rude

   c. Good job

2. What's a casual way to say "my bad"?

   a. ごめんなさい

   b. だいじょうぶ

   c. わるい

3. Which kanji means “apologize”?

   a. 感
   b. 謝
   c. 病

Bonus Prompt: Say this to yourself aloud, as practice: “ごめんなさい。しつれいしました。” (*go-me-na-sai, shi-tsu rei shi-ma-shita*). Feel how calm and grounding it is to apologize well.

Answers: 1–b, 2–c, 3–b

XP Earned: 20

You now know how to say “I’m sorry”—genuinely and with grace.

Badge Progress: Problem-Solver Pro – 2/5 Days Complete. You’re growing in emotional fluency, not just functional speech.

Final Thoughts

Apologies, when spoken well, are bridges. You now know how to speak from the heart in uncomfortable moments.

And guess what?

That's not beginner energy. That's leader energy. That's human energy.

Tomorrow, we shift from apology to understanding, learning how to say "I don't get it," and ask questions without fear.

See you for Day 23! Shall we keep going?

Scan to Listen

73%.....Complete!!

Day 23: Seek Clarifications

23

Mission: Ask When You Don't Understand

Here's the truth: You don't need to understand everything to belong. You just need to be brave enough to ask.

Today's mission is about reclaiming your power in the most practical way possible by learning how to say:

- "What does that mean?"
- "I don't understand."
- "Can you say it in English?"
- "Why?"

Because asking questions isn't a weakness; it's wisdom in motion.

Let's learn how to clarify and grow with confidence.

Phrases of the Day

Japanese	Pronunciation	Meaning
なに?	*na-ni?*	What?
わかりました	*wa-ka-ri-ma-shi-ta*	I understand / Got it
えいごで?	*ei-go de?*	In English?
どうして?	*dou-shi-te?*	Why?

How to Use Them

- ***なに? (na-ni?)***: Super simple: "What?" Can be sharp or soft—so use tone to match your mood. For clarity, try: "これは なに?" = "What is this?"
- ***わかりました (wa-ka-ri-ma-shi-ta)***: Polite way to say "I understand" or "Okay, got it." Use it after someone

explains something, and you truly get it. Also: "わかりません" = "I don't understand."

- えいごで? ***(ei-go de?)***: "In English?" This is your friendly lifeline when you're stuck. Say it with a smile. Bonus: Add "おねがいします" (*o-ne-gai shi-ma-su*) for extra politeness.
- どうして? ***(dou-shi-te?)***: "Why?" Use this when you want to understand more deeply. It's gentle curiosity, not confrontation.

Practice Tip: Say "わかりました" (*wa-ka-ri-ma-shi-ta*) like you're closing a conversation gently. Now say "どうして?" (*dou-shi-te*) with true curiosity, as if you want to understand, not challenge.

Kanji of the Day: 何

- **Meaning:** What
- **Reading:** なに (*na-ni*), なん (*nan*)
- **Mnemonic:** Imagine a person holding something unfamiliar and asking, "What's this?!"

Seen in:

- 何ですか (*nan de-su ka*) – What is it?
- 何時 (*nan-ji*) – What time?
- 何人 (*na-nnin*) – How many people?

Stroke Order

1. Left radical = "person"
2. Right = a complex symbol for questioning, like a bent head

Say "*nani*" and trace the shape slowly. This kanji is curiosity made visual.

Mini-Dialogue: Clarifying With Confidence

A: これは どういう いみ？（*Ko-re wa dou iu i-mi?* – What does this mean?）

B: たべものの なまえだよ。（*Ta-be-mo-no no na-mae da yo.* – It's the name of a food.）

A: あ、わかりました。ありがとう！（*Ah, wa-ka-ri-ma-shi-ta. A-ri-ga-tou!* – Oh, I got it. Thank you!）

B: わかって よかった！（*Wa-ka-tte yo-ka-tta!* – I'm glad you understood!）

Look at that! A soft moment of learning. No shame. Just connection.

Cultural Insight: The Power of "Wakarimasen"

In Japanese culture, it's common to pretend to understand to avoid inconvenience or seeming slow. But real learners? They say: "*Wakarimasen.*" "*Eigo de?*" "*Doushite?*"

These questions are gifts to your growth—and to the person helping you. Because clarity isn't rude; it's respectful.

- **Anime Moment:** In *Steins;Gate,* "何?"（*na-ni?*）drives curiosity and timelines. In *Erased,* every "どうして?"（*dou-shi-te*）uncovers truth. And in *My Hero Academia,* questions like "わかる?"（*wa-ka-ru?*）are how students grow.
- **Travel Tip:** Japanese teachers, tour guides, and shopkeepers often appreciate it when learners politely ask for clarity. Add a bow or smile, and you'll almost always get patient help.

Quick Quiz – 1 Minute

1. What does “どうして?” mean?

    a. Where?
    b. Why?
    c. Who?

2. What’s a polite way to say “I understand”?

    a. なに?
    b. えいごで?
    c. わかりました

3. Which kanji means “what”?

    a. 謝
    b. 何
    c. 感

Bonus Challenge: Say this full exchange: “すみません、えいごで おねがいします。” (*Su-mi-ma-sen, ei-go de o-ne-gai-shi-ma-su*). Polite. Kind. Empowered.

Answers: 1–b, 2–c, 3–b

XP Earned: 20

You just gave yourself the power to understand on your terms.

Badge Progress: Problem-Solver Pro – 3/5 Days Complete. You now ask boldly, kindly, and without shame.

Final Thoughts

Today's lesson wasn't flashy. But it was brave.

You now know how to:

- say "I don't understand."
- ask "What?"
- say "Why?" with care.
- ask for English without embarrassment.

That's how real learners learn. That's how real confidence is built.

Tomorrow, we'll take all that bravery and say the most powerful words of all: "Thank you."

See you for Day 24!

Scan to Listen

76%.....Complete!!

Day 24: Show Gratitude

24

Mission: Say "Thank You" With Heart

If there's one phrase you should never forget in any language, it's... Thank you.

Gratitude is a bridge. A healer. A moment that turns strangers into friends, helpers into heroes, and small gestures into lifelong memories.

In Japanese, there are many ways to say "thank you"—each with a slightly different tone, depth, and soul. Today, you'll learn how to express gratitude clearly, sweetly, and with cultural care.

Because "thank you" isn't just a phrase. It's a feeling—and now, it's your voice.

Phrases of the Day

Japanese	Pronunciation	Meaning
かんしゃします	*kan-sha shi-ma-su*	I'm deeply grateful
てつだってありがとう	*tet-su-da-tte a-ri-ga-tou*	Thanks for helping me
たのしかった	*ta-no-shi-ka-tta*	That was fun
またね	*ma-ta ne*	See you again / Later

How to Use Them

- **かんしゃします *(kan-sha shi-ma-su)***: This is serious gratitude—used when someone's done something truly meaningful. It's formal, deep, and best used when you feel moved or supported.

- てつだってありがとう ***(tet-su-da-tte a-ri-ga-tou)***: "Thanks for helping me." Use this after someone gives you directions, helps with your bag, or teaches you something new.
- たのしかった ***(ta-no-shi-ka-tta)***: "That was fun." Use it at the end of a great hangout, class, trip, or even a small chat. It leaves people feeling appreciated and seen.
- またね ***(ma-ta ne)***: Super casual "See you later." Use it with friends, classmates, or friendly strangers you hope to meet again. Feels warm and open.

Practice Tip: Say "かんしゃします" (*kan sha shi-ma-su*) slowly, like you're offering a bow with your voice. Then try "たのしかった～" (*ta-no-shi-ka-tta* ～) like you're smiling at a memory. That's how it lands softly.

Kanji of the Day: 感

- **Meaning:** Feeling / Emotion / Sense
- **Reading:** かん (*kan*)
- **Mnemonic:** A heart receiving signals—this kanji means to feel deeply.

Seen in:

- 感謝 (*kan-sha*) – gratitude
- 感じる (*kan-ji-ru*) – to feel
- 感動 (*kan-dou*) – emotional impact / being moved
- 感情 (*kan-jou*) – emotions

Stroke Order

1. Left radical = "heart"
2. Right = layers of action and reception

Say "*kan*" and trace it once slowly. Feel it. This kanji means your heart is listening.

Mini-Dialogue: Saying Thank You Naturally

A: ほんとうに、てつだってくれて ありがとう。(*Hon-tou ni, tet-su-da-tte ku-re-te a-ri-ga-tou.* – Really, thank you for helping me.)

B: だいじょうぶだよ〜 (*Dai-jou-bu da yo~* – It's all good!)

A: かんしゃします。たのしかった！ (*Kan-sha shi-ma-su. Ta-no-shi-ka-tta!* – I'm truly grateful. That was fun!)

B: またね！(*Ma-ta ne!* – See you later!)

This is how kindness ends—with warmth and presence. Practice this like you're saying goodbye after a meaningful day.

Cultural Insight: The Depth of "Arigatou"

You already know "ありがとう." (*a-ri-ga-tou*). But did you know the root comes from "ありがたし" (*a-ri-ga-ta-shi*), which means "rare" or "precious"?

In Japan, "thank you" isn't just polite. It means: "This mattered." "You didn't have to—but you did." "I see your effort."

- **Anime Moment:** In *Violet Evergarden,* gratitude becomes a life's calling. In *Spirited Away,* Chihiro bows deeply with "ありがとう" (*a-ri-ga-tou?*) as she says goodbye. In *Your Name,* the quietest "またね" (*ma-ta ne*) means everything.
- **Travel Tip:** You can use "ありがとう" (*a-ri-ga-tou*) almost anywhere. But when someone really helps you? Try: " ほんとうに、かんしゃしてます。" (*Hon-tou ni, kan sha shi-te-ma-su*). It lands like gold.

Quick Quiz – 1 Minute

1. What does "またね" mean?
    a. Let's eat
    b. I'm sorry
    c. See you again
2. Which phrase means "Thanks for helping me"?
    a. てつだってありがとう
    b. ごめんなさい
    c. わかりました
3. Which kanji means "feeling"?
    a. 病
    b. 感
    c. 力

Bonus Prompt: Say this to yourself: "かんしゃします。たのしかった!" (*Kan-sha shi-ma-su. Ta-no-shi-ka-tta!*) Let it feel like the end of a beautiful day.

Answers: 1–c, 2–a, 3–b

XP Earned: 20

You now speak gratitude—with soul and sincerity.

Badge Progress: Problem-Solver Pro – 4/5 Days Complete. One more day and you finish your week with power and peace.

Final Thoughts

Today's lesson was about the most powerful sentence you can carry anywhere: "Thank you."

You now know how to say:

- Thanks for helping.
- That was fun.
- I feel gratitude.
- See you again.

That's not just good Japanese. That's good humanity.

Tomorrow, we close out this week with a full-circle review—and your final badge for strength under pressure.

See you for Day 25!

Scan to Listen

80%.....Complete!!

Day 25: Speak Like a Leader

Mission: Respond With Calm. Speak With Care.

You made it. Not just to the end of Week 5, but through the kind of Japanese that really matters.

This wasn't about shopping or sightseeing. This was about emotional fluency. The kind that shows up when someone's hurt. Or confused. Or scared. Or grateful.

This is the language of real life. And now you speak it.

The Quiet Power of Language

Fluent doesn't mean perfect. Fluent means present. Calm. Capable. Caring.

This week, you practiced:

- Asking for help, and offering it.
- Saying "I'm sorry" without shame.
- Asking questions without panic.
- Giving thanks that feels real.

That's leadership. In any language.

Scenario Challenge: You're the Calm Voice

Imagine you're with a friend in Japan and they fall ill. They panic—you don't.

You take a breath and say: 「だいじょうぶ。びょういんはどこですか?」(*Dai-jou-bu. Byou in wa do-ko-de-su ka?*)

When they apologize, you answer:「だいじょうぶです。しんぱいしないで。」(*Dai-jou-bu-de-su. Shin-pai-shi-nai-de*)

You're not the most fluent speaker in the room. But you're the one who kept everyone grounded. That's fluency in action.

Emotional Scripts for Real Life

Here are phrases that carry you through difficult moments—not with perfection, but with presence:

- ごめんなさい (*Go-me-na-sai*)
- だいじょうぶ? (*Dai-jou-bu?*)
- わかりました (*Wa-ka-ri-ma-shi-ta*)
- えいごで? (*Ei go de?*)
- かんしゃします (*Kan-sha shi-ma-su*)

Say them out loud. Now try this: Say one as a whisper. Then say it as if someone truly needs to hear it.

That's emotional range. That's care, in your voice.

Cultural Insight: Grace Under Pressure

In Japanese culture, responding calmly—even under stress—is highly respected. A deep bow. A soft "しつれい." (*shi-tsu-rei*). A quiet "かんしゃしてます." (*kan-sha shi-te-ma-su*) These aren't small things. They signal character.

This week, you began to embody that.

Anime Moment: In *Violet Evergarden,* an apology becomes a life-changing letter. In *Demon Slayer,* "だいじょうぶ" (*dai-jou-bu*) doesn't just reassure; it restores. And in *Spirited Away,* one kind word shifts an entire journey.

You're learning not just what to say, but how to mean it.

Final Prompt: Say It With Soul

Write or voice this sentence:「ごめんなさい。でも、かんしゃしてます。」(*Go-me-na-sai. De-mo, kan sha shi-te-ma-su.*)

Now try one of your own. Make it reflect something real inside you.

XP Earned: 20

You completed Week 5: Practical Scenarios. That's real-life Japanese fluency unlocked.

Badge Earned: Problem-Solver Pro

You now lead with grace, even when life gets messy.

You Now Know How To

- Ask for help without hesitation.
- Apologize with honesty.
- Speak in uncertainty.
- Thank with heart.
- Respond with clarity, even when unsure.

You didn't just learn "practical phrases." You learned how to be steady in a second language.

Week 5: Final Gem – The Gem of Belonging

You've made it.

Over the past 5 weeks, you've learned, practiced, laughed, hesitated, retried, and grown. You've used Japanese in a way that feels real, not just as a study, but as a part of your world.

This final gem is about belonging—to the journey, to the culture, and to your own evolving self.

Gem of Belonging Earned

You now have all 5 gems. But more importantly, you've proven something to yourself: You can do this. And you did. Now it's time for your final quest. Achieving the Quest Master Badge!

Final Thoughts

I know this wasn't the easiest week. But it was the most powerful.

You're not just someone who can order ramen or say their name. You're someone who can say:

"I don't understand—but I'm here." "I'm sorry—but I'll do better." "I'm grateful—truly."

That's leader energy. That's connection. That's you.

Next up? Week 6: Mastery and Celebration. Let's take all the pieces and turn them into something unstoppable.

Ready for the final week? Let's go!

Scan to Listen

83%.....Complete!!

Personal Phrase Journal

Week 5: Practical Scenarios

Focus: Apologies, asking for help, and emotional control in Japanese.

A Phrase That Grounded Me

Phrase: ______________________________

When I imagined using it:

____

A Phrase I'd Use in a Tough Situation

Phrase: ______________________________

What it would help with:

____

A Way I Expressed Gratitude

Japanese: ______________________________

Romaji: ______________________________

Why I chose this phrase: ______________________________

Next Week's Intention

- ❑ Stay calm while speaking
- ❑ Use "thank you" with real feeling
- ❑ Memorize a crisis-support phrase

Week 6: Mastery and Celebration

From Learner to Speaker—Your Japanese Journey in Motion

You've come so far.

What started as "*Konnichiwa*" is now full conversations. What began with bowing and hesitation is now fluency, with confidence, connection, and compassion.

This week? You're living it.

Welcome to Week 6: Mastery and Celebration—a final set of missions designed to reinforce everything you've learned and let you experience how ready you truly are.

Why This Week Matters

You didn't just memorize words. You built muscle memory. You trained your ear. You spoke with your heart.

And now, you get to own it in practical, powerful ways—with simulated real-world experiences like:

- Ordering food at a Japanese restaurant

- Talking with a new friend at an anime convention
- Handling a social mix-up with grace
- Saying goodbye··· with gratitude

Each day this week gives you:

- Familiar phrases
- Reinforced kanji
- Real-world mini-dialogues
- A little challenge to test your strength
- A celebration of YOU

Because this is the week you realize··· You're not a beginner anymore.

How the Final Week Works

You've already done the heavy lifting. This week is all about confidence and reflection.

Each day includes:

- A realistic mission scenario
- Phrases you've already learned (with a few bonus expressions!)
- Kanji review from previous weeks
- Dialogue examples that feel like real life
- A recap-style quiz to test how far you've come
- Encouragement, humor, and a moment of pride
- XP toward your final badge: Quest Master

You'll review 20+ phrases and 22 kanji you've already learned—but this time, you'll use them in context.

No guesswork. No hand-holding. Just YOU—speaking Japanese with flow.

Cultural Reflection: The Journey Is the Reward

Japanese culture honors process. Perfection isn't expected. Effort is everything.

There's even a phrase for it: 継続は力なり (*kei-zo-ku wa chi-ka-ra na-ri*) "Consistency becomes strength."

You didn't become fluent overnight. You became fluent through rhythm, emotion, and curiosity. And now… you're not just a learner. You're part of a language, a culture, and a community.

That's what you did here. Quiet power. Loud joy.

Final Thoughts

This week is your final lap—but it's also your first real run.

You'll:

- Reflect on what you've learned.
- Use everything in real, emotional moments.
- Surprise yourself with how natural Japanese feels in your mouth.
- Celebrate not just the language, but the life you've created around it.

And this final week will be a bit tricky, as you must put your knowledge into action and use it to decipher some sentences that you'll find during these days.

So get ready. This week, your Japanese journey goes live.

First up: Day 26: Travel Scenario—trains, tickets, and the thrill of moving through Japan like a local.

Are you ready to begin your final quest? Let's go earn that Quest Master badge!

Day 26: Travel Scenario 26

Mission: Buy a Ticket and Ride Like a Local

You step off the plane. The signs are in kanji. The station is buzzing. You're carrying your bag, your excitement… and your Japanese.

You spot the ticket machine, glance at the schedule, and take a deep breath. You got this.

Today's mission is to simulate a real travel experience—from buying a train ticket to asking where the station is. You'll be using phrases you already know, kanji you can now recognize, and the confidence you've built over the past five weeks.

Let's go on your first Japanese adventure—on your terms.

Phrases of the Day

Japanese	Pronunciation	Meaning
えきはどこ?	*e-ki wa do-ko?*	Where's the station?
いくらですか?	*i-ku-ra de-su ka?*	How much is it?
これください	*ko-re ku-da-sai*	This one, please
みずください	*mi-zu ku-da-sai*	Water, please

Bonus Phrase: 切符をください (*ki-ppu o ku-da-sai*): A ticket, please

You've used every one of these before, but now you'll use them together.

Kanji of the Day: 駅 – 円 – 水

Kanji	Reading	Meaning
駅	*e-ki*	Station
円	*en*	Yen (currency)
水	*mi-zu*	Water

Mini Challenge: Can you read this sentence? 駅で 水を 買いました。(*E-ki de mi-zu o kai-ma-shi-ta.* – I bought water at the station.)

You know all the kanji now. That's a full sentence. That's you.

Real-World Mini-Dialogue

Let's walk through a realistic train station moment:

You: すみません、駅はどこ? (*Su-mi-ma-sen, eki wa doko?*)

Stranger: あっちです。(*At-chi-de-su*)

You: ありがとう!(*A-ri-ga-tou!*)

[At the ticket counter]

You: 東京まで、切符をください。(*To-kyo ma-de, ki-ppu o ku-da-sai.*)

Staff: はい。500円です。(*Ha-i. 500-En-de-su.*)

You: はい、これください。みずも、ください。(*Ha-i, ko-re ku-da-sai. Mi-zu mo, ku-da-sai.*)

Staff: ありがとうございます! (*A-ri-ga-tou-go-zai-ma-su!*)

Boom. That's real. You're speaking. You're living the language.

Cultural Insight: Train Culture in Japan

Japanese train stations are beautifully organized, but also fast-paced. You'll often hear polite phrases like:

- “すみません” (*Su-mi-ma-sen* / Excuse me) as people move past
- “ありがとうございます” (*A-ri-ga-tou go-zai-ma-su* / Thank you) from the staff when handing tickets
- “ご注意ください” over the speakers (*Go chui ku-da-sai* / Please be careful)

You'll also see vending machines near the platforms, and bowing as a subtle thank-you, even between strangers.

- **Anime Moment:** In *Your Name,* train stations are where fate shifts. In *5 Centimeters Per Second,* goodbyes happen at platforms.
- **Travel Tip:** If you can ask for a ticket and confirm the price, you can travel anywhere in Japan. You're not just a visitor. You're part of the flow.

Quick Quiz – 1 Minute

1. What does “切符をください” mean?
    a. Please give me a coin
    b. Please give me a ticket
    c. Where is the ticket?
2. What's the meaning of “駅” ?
    a. Water
    b. Food
    c. Station
3. Which kanji means yen/currency?
    a. 円
    b. 名
    c. 行

Bonus Prompt: Write this full sentence in romaji: "*Eki wa do-ko? Ki-ppu o ku-da-sai. I-ku-ra de-su ka?*" Practice it aloud like a role-play. This is real-world readiness.

Answers: 1–b, 2–c, 3–a

XP Earned: 20

You just passed your first Japanese travel simulation.

Badge Progress: Quest Master – 1/5 Days Complete. You're no longer guessing. You're navigating with skill and respect.

Final Thoughts

You didn't just review today—you moved. You:

- Asked where to go.
- Understood the response.
- Ordered, paid, and received—all in Japanese.

That's your voice in motion. That's mastery.

Tomorrow, you step into a new kind of space—one that feels like home:

Anime Fandom!

Get ready for Day 27!

Scan to Listen

86%.....Complete!!

Day 27: Anime Fan Scenario

27

Mission: Speak With Passion—Like the Anime Fan You Are

You're at your first anime convention in Tokyo. Cosplayers everywhere. Merch tables. A voice actor panel is in the distance. You walk through the crowd, and someone cosplaying your favorite character waves at you.

It's time.

Today's mission puts your fandom front and center. You'll practice key phrases from your anime-focused week and bring them to life in a high-energy, expressive, and fan-filled setting.

Let's channel your inner protagonist—and speak with joy and courage.

Phrases of the Day

Japanese	Pronunciation	Meaning
げんき?	*gen-ki?*	You good? / How are you?
すごい!	*su-goi!*	Amazing! / Wow!
かわいい	*ka-waii*	Cute!
すき	*su-ki*	I like (you/it)

Bonus Phrase: オタクです！(*o-ta-ku de-su!* / I'm a fan!)

You already know these, but now you get to use them in conversation that's fast, fun, and full of emotion.

Practice Tip: Say each one with an expressive tone and body language.

- "すごーーい!!" (*Su-goi!*) = starry eyes

- “すき!” (*su-ki!*) = soft smile
- “げんき?” (*Gen-ki?*) = friendly wave

Anime is feeling-forward. You've got this.

Kanji of the Day: 気 – 心 – 愛

Kanji	Reading	Meaning
気	*ki*	Spirit / Energy
心	*ko-ko-ro*	Heart / Emotion
愛	*ai*	Love

These kanji live in anime. You'll spot them in logos, names, powers, and poems.

Challenge: Can you read this phrase? 心から、すきです。(*Ko-ko-ro ka-ra, su-ki de-su.* – I love it from my heart.)

That's the language of fandom. That's the language of you.

Real-World Mini-Dialogue: Fan to Fan

You (cosplaying as Naruto): よっ!そのコスプレ、すごい! (*Yo! So-no ko-su-pu-re, su-goi!*)

Them (dressed as Nezuko): ありがとう〜かわいいって言われた〜 (*A-ri-ga-tou ~ ka wa ii-tte i-wa re-ta*)

You: すき!わたしもオタクです! (*Su-ki! Wa-ta-shi mo o-ta-ku-de-su!*)

Them: げんき?どのアニメが一番? (*Gen-ki? Do-no a-ni-me ga i-chi-ban?*)

You: 今?「呪術廻戦」かな〜 (*I-ma? `Ju-jut-su Ma-wa-ri-sen ka na ~*)

This is what you've been preparing for. Real moments. Real fans. Real Japanese.

Cultural Insight: Otaku Power, Real Respect

In Japan, being an otaku (オタク) is no longer niche; it's an identity. And fan spaces are safe zones to express love for anime, games, idols, and beyond.

- **Anime Moment:** In *K-On!*, connection happens over "すきなバンド." (*su-ki-na ban-do*). In *Ouran High School Host Club,* suki starts chaotic romance. In *Konosuba,* every character shouts "すごい!" (*su-goi!*) at magic and mayhem.
- **Fan Tip:** Use "すき" with context! Say: "このキャラ、すき。" (*ko-no kya-ra su-ki* / I love this character.) "このアニメ、すき!" (*ko-no a-ni-me su-ki* / I love this anime!). It's personal and joyful—just like you.

Quick Quiz – 1 Minute

1. What does "すごい!" mean?
   a. Sad
   b. Amazing!
   c. Tired
2. What's the meaning of "オタクです"?
   a. I'm late
   b. I'm shy
   c. I'm a fan / otaku
3. Which kanji means "heart/emotion"?
   a. 愛
   b. 心
   c. 気

Bonus Prompt: Say this out loud: "オタクです。すごいアニメ、すき!" (*O-ta-ku-de-su. Ga a-ni-me, su-ki!*) Feel the energy. Feel seen.

Answers: 1–b, 2–c, 3–b

XP Earned: 20

You've completed your first fan-based conversation. You now speak the language of connection and the culture you love.

Badge Progress: Quest Master – 2/5 Days Complete. You're not just fluent. You're fluent with flair.

Final Thoughts

Today, you proved something huge:

You don't just understand Japanese. You feel it. You live it. You connect through it.

This wasn't just practice. It was expression.

Tomorrow, we slow down··· and warm up a new space: casual, cozy conversation with friends.

Let's move into Day 28!

Scan to Listen

90%.....Complete!!

Day 28: Social Scenario

28

Mission: Connect, Chat, and Just Be You

You're sitting under paper lanterns at a summer festival. Laughter. Yakisoba. Fireworks warming the sky. A new friend turns to you with a smile.

"O-genki?"

You smile back. "*Tanoshii. Namae wa?*"

This is what today's mission is about: flow. You've already learned the phrases. Now, it's about using them without thinking, just like you would with your real friends.

Let's step into your first full social moment. Not a test. Not a task. Just you—relaxed, expressive, and completely conversational.

Phrases of the Day

Japanese	Pronunciation	Meaning
なまえは?	*na-mae wa?*	What's your name?
おげんき?	*o-gen-ki?*	How are you?
きれい	*ki-rei*	Beautiful
いいね!	*ii ne!*	Nice! / That's great!

Bonus Phrase: にほんすき? (*ni-hon su-ki?* / Do you like Japan?)

These are phrases you already own—now they're becoming reflexes.

Practice Tip: Try saying each one while imagining the face of someone you like. This isn't grammar; it's relationship building.

Kanji of the Day: 名 – 美 – 行

Kanji	Reading	Meaning
名	*na / mei*	Name
美	*bi*	Beauty
行	*iku / kou*	Go / Travel / Hang out

Read this? 行こう、[Name]！いいね？ (Let's go, [Name]! Sound good?) Yep. You're not studying anymore. You're speaking.

Real-World Mini-Dialogue: Festival Friend Chat

You: おげんき？ (How are you?)

Friend: うん、たのしいね～ (Yeah, this is fun.)

You: なまえは？ (What's your name?)

Friend: わたしは リナ。(I'm Rina.)

You: きれいな なまえ！ にほんすき？ (Beautiful name! Do you like Japan?)

Friend: うん、すき！また あそぼうね！ (Yeah, I love it! Let's hang out again!)

THIS is fluency: calm, curious, kind conversation. No pressure. Just presence.

Cultural Insight: Relationships Built Softly

Japanese small talk values comfort over speed. It's not about filling space; it's about sensing tone, making others feel safe, and letting warmth lead.

Phrases like:

- "いいね！" – affirm and build connection.
- "きれい" – offer kindness without tension.

» “にほんすき?” – invite deeper curiosity.

- **Anime Moment:** In *Yuru Camp,* friendship grows from weather talk. In *Clannad,* casual phrases soften heavy hearts. In *Horimiya,* “いいね!”（*ii-ne!*）becomes a small, steady thread of intimacy.
- **Real-Life Tip:** In Japan, one compliment + one question = magic. Try: “なまえは?きれい!”（*na-mae wa? ki-rei!*）Or “にほんすき?またね?”（*ni hon su-ki? Ma-ta ne?*）

It lands with heart.

Quick Quiz – 1 Minute

1. What does “なまえは?” mean?
   a. How are you?
   b. What's your name?
   c. Where are you from?
2. What's the meaning of “いいね”?
   a. I don't know
   b. Nice!
   c. Never mind
3. Which kanji means “beauty”?
   a. 美
   b. 名
   c. 感

Bonus Prompt: Try writing: “おげんき?またね。”（*O gen-ki? Ma-ta ne.*）Simple. Friendly. Perfectly human.

Answers: 1–b, 2–b, 3–a

XP Earned: 20

You just completed your first natural, low-pressure Japanese conversation.

Badge Progress: Quest Master – 3/5 Days Complete. Now you're speaking with softness, not just skill.

Final Thoughts

This wasn't about grammar. It was about rhythm. Realness. Relationship.

You just:

- Checked in.
- Gave a compliment.
- Asked a question.
- Said goodbye.

All in Japanese. All with heart.

Tomorrow? We bring all your worlds together in one emotional, high-utility mission: Mixed Scenario, the final test before celebration. Let's keep going!

Scan to Listen

93%.....Complete!!

Day 29: Mixed Scenario 29

Mission: React, Respond, and Recover With Confidence

You're in a cozy ramen shop. You bumped into someone by accident. You forgot how to say something in Japanese. Then the chef gives you a free side dish, your favorite.

One minute, you're flustered. The next, you're smiling.

This is language in real life. Messy. Beautiful. Dynamic.

Today's mission is to blend all your lessons—asking for clarity, saying sorry, expressing gratitude, and talking about food. All at once.

Phrases of the Day

Japanese	Pronunciation	Meaning
ごめんなさい	*go-men na-sai*	I'm sorry
なに?	*na-ni?*	What?
またね	*ma-ta ne*	See you again
おいしい!	*oi-shii!*	Delicious!

Bonus Phrase: ほんとうに、ありがとう (*hon-tou ni, a-ri-ga-tou* / Really, thank you)

These phrases are your Swiss Army knife; they adapt to any situation with grace.

Practice Tip: Try saying: "ごめんなさい… なに?… おいしい! ほんとうに、ありがとう。" (*Go-me-na-sai... na-ni? Oi-shii! Hon-tou ni, a-ri-ga-tou.*) Can you feel the story arc in just those words?

Kanji of the Day: 謝 – 何 – 食

Kanji	Reading	Meaning
謝	*sha / a-ya-ma*	Apologize
何	*na-ni / nan*	What
食	*sho-ku / ta-be*	Eat / Food

Mini-Challenge: Can you read this? 何これ? 食べてもいい? (What is this? Can I eat it?) Yep. That's survival and celebration in one sentence.

Real-World Mini-Dialogue: Restaurant Mix-Up

You (accidentally bump into someone): ごめんなさい! (I'm so sorry!)

Them: だいじょうぶです〜 (It's okay!)

You (receiving a dish you didn't order): えっ? なに? (Huh? What's this?)

Chef: サービスです〜 (It's on the house!)

You: ほんとうに、ありがとう!おいしい!! (Thank you so much! It's delicious!!)

Them (leaving): またね! (See you again!)

You: またね〜たのしかった! (See you! That was fun!)

This is the most powerful kind of fluency: Not perfect, but alive. Honest. Human.

Cultural Insight: Grace in the Unexpected

In Japanese culture, your tone matters more than your words.

» Say ごめんなさい (*go-me-na-sai*) sincerely and you'll always be forgiven.

» Ask なに? (*na-ni?*) politely, and you'll almost always be helped.

» Smile with おいしい! (*oi-shii!*) and people light up.

- **Anime Moment:** In Food Wars, "おいしい!!" (*oi-shii!*) literally explodes with flavor. In Spirited Away, small thanks soften big fear. In Fruits Basket, recovery moments matter more than perfect ones.
- **Travel Tip:** If you panic or freeze, say: "ごめんなさい、えいごで?" (*Go-me-na-sai ei-go de?*) That's calm. Respectful. It always works.

Quick Quiz – 1 Minute

1. What does "ほんとうに、ありがとう" mean?

    a. Where is it?

    b. I really love you

    c. Truly, thank you

2. What's the meaning of "おいしい"?

    a. Scary

    b. Delicious

    c. Difficult

3. Which kanji means "food/eat"?

    a. 食

    b. 愛

    c. 行

Bonus Prompt: Say this out loud, like you're in a real ramen shop: "ごめんなさい… なに?… おいしい!ほんとうに、ありがとう。" (*Go-me-na-sai... na-ni? Oi-shii! Hon-tou ni, a-ri-gatou*) That's story in five words. You're ready.

Answers: 1–c, 2–b, 3–a

XP Earned: 20

You just faced chaos with calm. That's conversational agility.

Badge Progress: Quest Master – 4/5 Days Complete. You're now fluent under pressure.

Final Thoughts

You just combined:

- An apology
- A question
- A thank-you
- A goodbye
- A compliment

All in one real-world moment.

You're not reciting anymore. You're responding. Recovering. Relating.

This is it. Tomorrow is your final mission.

Your victory lap. Your moment of reflection. Your Quest Master badge is waiting.

See you on Day 30!

Scan to Listen

96%.....Complete!!

Day 30: You Did It. You Are It

Mission: Honor Your Voice, Celebrate Your Growth, and Step Into What's Next

Most people never start. Fewer stay with it. But you did something rare: You stayed consistent. You stayed curious. And now, you speak Japanese.

Not perfectly. Not like a textbook. But like you. With feeling. With flow. With heart.

The Power of Small, Brave Moments

You didn't get here by cramming kanji or chasing fluency in one giant leap. You got here by showing up—10 minutes at a time.

That's fluency. Not speed. Not perfection. Just honest effort, over time. Today is your day to feel proud. To mark the moment.

Ritual: Your Fluency Ceremony

Let's close this chapter with intention.

Step 1: Speak From the Heart

Choose any 4 phrases from the book that feel like you.

Say them aloud slowly, as if you're writing your name in the sky.

Say them again—like you're in Tokyo, meeting someone who matters.

Say them a third time—like you're speaking to yourself, with love.

Step 2: Connect With Meaning

Pick 4 kanji you connected with the most. Draw them big. Say their names. Speak their meanings.

Then say: "I carry these meanings now." Because you do.

Step 3: Write Your Graduation Line

What would you say to your Day 1 self? Write it down. Speak it aloud. Example: "You were scared, but you began anyway. Look where it took you." "Thank you for trying. We speak Japanese now."

That's your 証 (*a-ka-shi*)—your proof.

Final Scene: The Moment You Became Conversational

You're at a small café in Japan. Someone bumps your chair, turns, and smiles.

Them: 「すみません！ だいじょうぶ？」(Excuse me! Are you okay?)

You: 「うん、だいじょうぶ。ありがとう！」(Yeah, I'm okay. Thanks!)

Them: 「あなたの日本語、すてきだね。」(Your Japanese is lovely.)

You: 「ほんとう？ うれしい…またね？」(Really? I'm happy… See you again?)

Them: 「またね！」(See you!)

That's it. That's the moment.

Cultural Insight: You're No Longer an Outsider

When you said your first "こんにちは," (*ko-ni-chi-wa*), you crossed a line—from curiosity to courage. And every moment since, you've been building a bridge.

Now you:

- Understand nuance.
- Respond with care.
- Laugh, cheer, and ask for help—in Japanese.
- Know how to make someone feel seen with just a few words.

That's not "beginner Japanese." That's your Japanese.

Anime Moment: In Your Name, the words that matter most don't always come right away—but they arrive when you're ready. Today, you don't just know the words, you carry the weight they hold.

Badge Earned: QUEST MASTER

You started from zero. Now, you:

- Hold a conversation.
- Read key kanji.
- Express emotion, ask for help, celebrate joy, and invite connection.

You're conversational. You're confident. You're ready.

Final Words

This is not the end. This is a beginning disguised as a finish line.

You now have the tools. The rest? It's simply repetition, curiosity, and continued joy.

So here's what I want you to remember:

You can speak.

You are heard.

You belong.

またね (See you again). ありがとう (Thank you). おめでとうございます (Congratulations).

Scan to Listen

100%.....Complete!!

Personal Phrase Journal

Week 6: Mastery and Celebration

Focus: Confidence, favorite expressions, forward momentum.

My Signature Phrase

The one I now "own":

____

How I'll keep using it:

____

A Phrase I'd Teach a Friend

Phrase: ______________________________

Why I'd share it:

____

If My Japanese Journey Had a Title

It would be: ______________________________

Because: ______________________________

Beyond This Book…

- ❑ I'll study grammar
- ❑ Join a meetup / Discord
- ❑ Start writing short stories
- ❑ Keep saying a little every day
- ❑ Other:

You Speak More Than You Know

If you've filled even a few of these pages, you've done something powerful: You didn't just learn Japanese. You lived it.

You noticed what made you laugh. You reflected when something clicked. You chose words that represent who you are and how you want to connect.

That's fluency, not the kind that's tested, but the kind that's felt.

This doesn't mark the end of your journey. It's a snapshot of who you are right now, someone brave enough to try, curious enough to reflect, and strong enough to keep going.

So return to these pages when you need a boost. Add to them when a new phrase lights you up. And let this journal remind you: You don't just speak Japanese. You've made it your own.

またね。がんばってね。(See you soon. Good luck!)

Conclusion: From Zero to Connection

Remember when you opened this book?

You might've been curious. Or nervous. Or both. Maybe you weren't sure how far 10 minutes a day could really take you.

But look at you now.

Over the past 6 weeks, you've:

- Learned 120+ practical Japanese words and phrases.
- Mastered 22 foundational kanji, stroke by stroke.
- Recognized the difference between hiragana, katakana, and kanji.
- Built confidence with daily dialogues and real-life scenarios.
- Connected with the culture through anime moments, etiquette, and travel tips.
- Collected 5 symbolic gems that represent your growth.

And most importantly, you've spoken real Japanese.

That's progress and transformation.

You've gone from flipping flashcards in doubt to understanding how the language actually works. You've practiced how to greet someone, ask for help, make a new friend, order food, and even reflect on your journey in Japanese.

You've started listening differently. Speaking with more intention. Writing with more care. And that means: You're a Japanese communicator in the making.

What You've Gained

This wasn't just a crash course. It was a commitment to curiosity. And along the way, you built something far deeper than language.

Here's what you now carry with you:

Confidence

You learned to open your mouth and speak—even when your voice trembled. You practiced even when you weren't sure. You made mistakes and kept going.

That's courage. That's the kind of confidence that shows up outside of language, too.

Cultural Insight

You didn't just study how to say "excuse me" or "please." You learned when and why those words matter.

You began to understand how Japanese speakers navigate politeness, emotion, and connection. You stepped into a culture of grace, presence, and care, and you honored it.

Real Fluency Foundations

You're not just memorizing. You're using Japanese to:

- Greet people.

- Make requests.
- Express joy, surprise, or gratitude.
- Handle confusion or emergencies.
- Cheer someone on or tell someone they matter.

You now have a tool kit of phrases and kanji not in your head, but in your hands.

A Growth Mindset

Every time you paused and tried again··· Every time you forgot and forgave yourself··· Every time you spoke out loud instead of just thinking about it···

You proved something: You're learning Japanese, and learning to trust yourself.

A Final Word From the Author

This book was never about being "impressive."

It was written to be warm. Useful. Human.

I wanted it to feel like a friend sitting next to you, not a teacher hovering over you. Because I know what it's like to want something so badly, and feel like it's too far away.

I also know the secret: The people who become fluent aren't the fastest. They're the most consistent. They come back. Again. And again. And again.

So if you've made it here—if you've read these words—you already belong to that group.

Japanese isn't just a skill. It's a door to connection, culture, identity, and imagination.

You've already stepped through it.

You're a Speaker Now

Yes, you. You're not a "maybe someday" learner anymore.

You've greeted strangers. You've made friends in your mind and your notebook. You've apologized, asked questions, and said "またね" (*ma-ta ne*) with meaning.

You may not feel fluent yet, but you're fluent in courage. And that's what matters most.

Take a moment to breathe it in.

You did this. From your first uncertain "*konnichiwa*" ··· To the smile that came with your first "やった！" ··· (*Ya-tta*) to now, this moment.

You're a speaker. A fan who now speaks the language of their favorite worlds. A traveler with more tools than you had 30 days ago. A human with something real to say.

And guess what?

Your journey is just beginning.

One Last Time

またね (*Ma-ta ne*) — See you again.

ありがとう (*A-ri-ga-tou*) — Thank you.

がんばってね (*Gan-ba-tte ne*) — Keep going.

Your voice matters. In any language.

And now··· It's just getting started.

From zero to conversational—mission complete.

★ EXCLUSIVE FREE READER BONUSES ★

Congratulations on your commitment to learning Japanese!

I've created special bonuses just for you. These bonuses are my way of supporting your Japanese learning journey. I hope they help!

Arigatou gozaimasu!

- ✔ Secret Bonus Quest to push you beyond beginner level.
- ✔ Quest Master Certificate: Your achievement badge to celebrate success.
- ✔ Flashcards

SCAN THE QR CODE TO DOWNLOAD COMPLEMENTARY BONUSES FOR YOUR QUEST

A Letter to Your Day One Self

Dear Day One Me,

Hey. Remember me? I'm the version of you who's on the other side of this book, the one who now gets it. The one who can read, speak, and understand a language that once looked like a wall of beautiful but totally confusing symbols.

Wild, right?

I still remember what it felt like at the start. That blank notebook. The flashcards. The slightly panicked feeling of: "Wait··· is that a letter or a picture?" And the quiet doubt whispering: What if this is too hard for me?

Spoiler: It wasn't. It was hard at times, sure—but you did it.

You stuck around when things got confusing. You kept going when it felt awkward. You started where you were—with nothing but curiosity and a tiny bit of courage—and now? You're using Japanese.

Let that sink in.

You Showed Up, Even When You Felt Lost

On day one, you probably had no idea where this would go. You might have worried:

- *Am I too old to learn a new language?*
- *What if I'm not consistent enough?*
- *What if I never remember which が is which?*

But you showed up anyway. Maybe for five minutes. Maybe for a day, then took a break, then came back. But you came back.

That's the part I want to celebrate most: You didn't give up on yourself.

You made peace with sounding silly sometimes. And little by little, symbol by symbol, word by word, you started to build something real.

You Didn't Just Memorize; You Connected

At first, Japanese might have felt like a code to crack. But somewhere along the way, it started to feel like a conversation.

You stopped just memorizing sounds. You started recognizing rhythm, meaning, and nuance.

You didn't just learn "どうもありがとうございます"; you learned how it feels when someone says it to you with a bow. You didn't just learn "かわいい"; you started feeling it every time you saw something adorable and just had to say it out loud. You didn't just translate; you started thinking in Japanese, even just a little.

That's more than language acquisition. That's cultural connection. That's growth.

Remember When You Couldn't Even Read Hiragana?

Let's take a second to appreciate that. Hiragana—those soft, curvy characters that once looked like beautiful scribbles—they used to be a mystery.

And now?

You read them. You write them. You recognize them out in the wild like old friends.

The same with Katakana—those sharper, louder characters that seemed impossible to remember—now you see them in anime credits, on menus, in video games··· and you get it.

Oh, and Kanji?

You used to think you'd never learn even one. Now you've got a growing list in your head. You may not know all of them (nobody does!), but you understand their power. And every one you learn unlocks a little more of the world.

Don't gloss over that. That's huge.

You Built Your Own System

This wasn't just about following a book. You made it personal.

You wrote down phrases that meant something to you. You practiced talking about your favorite things. You figured out which learning methods clicked for your brain and tossed out what didn't work. You kept a journal. You practiced with your own voice. You owned this process.

You made this language yours. Not perfectly—but authentically.

And that's what makes it stick. Not rigid rules, but personal connection.

You Messed Up, and That's What Made You Stronger

Let's not pretend it was all smooth.

You probably said something weird by accident. Mixed up words. Forgot obvious stuff. Stared at the same sentence five times before it made sense.

And guess what?

That's where the learning actually happened.

Those moments—the awkward, clumsy, "oops" moments—are what built your foundation. You didn't fail. You figured it out. You flexed your brain. You adjusted. You laughed it off. You kept going.

And that's the difference between people who learn a language and people who just wish they could.

You Can Do More Than You Think

Right now, you might still feel like you're "not fluent"—and maybe you're not. But pause. Look back.

You can:

- Recognize kanji and understand how they work.
- Hold simple conversations.
- Talk about your day, your food, your likes, and dislikes.
- Order ramen in Japanese if you had to.
- Sing along to parts of your favorite anime opening, even if you're a beat behind.

That's not nothing. That's not "beginner energy." That's a real skill. One that only a small percentage of people stick with long enough to build.

And now you get to keep building it from here.

You Get to Decide What's Next

The best part?

You're not "finished." You're just equipped.

Now, you get to choose what kind of Japanese speaker you want to be:

- The traveler who uses Japanese to explore cities, temples, and hidden ramen shops
- The anime fan who can finally turn off the subtitles
- The pen pal who connects with people halfway across the world
- The learner who keeps mastering kanji just because they can

Or just the person who wanted to prove to themselves they could do this—and did.

There's no one right way to continue. Whatever you choose is valid, and possible, and yours.

And If You Ever Forget How Far You've Come⋯

Open this letter again. Look at your first notebook. Read one of the first phrases you learned and smile at how small it seemed then.

You didn't just learn a language. You expanded your world. You built trust with yourself. You became the kind of person who says:

"Yeah, I didn't know anything at first⋯ but I figured it out."

That's not just about Japanese. That's about you.

You're resourceful. Curious. Resilient. You're the kind of person who keeps going. Who makes progress when nobody's watching. Who creates connection across cultures, across countries, across fear.

You're a learner. A beginner who became a communicator.

And that Day One version of you?

They'd be so proud.

おめでとう。You did it. And you're just getting started.

With love,

Your Future Self—the one who speaks Japanese now.

90+ Everyday Japanese Phrases

The phrases in this section were chosen with care to help you do exactly that: Connect with real people in real situations. From heartfelt greetings to playful expressions, polite requests to everyday interactions, this list gives you over 90+ useful, natural phrases you can start using immediately.

Even if you're chatting with friends about your favorite anime or simply trying to order a meal, these phrases are your passport to meaningful conversations. Say them out loud. Feel them. Make them yours.

As you've just seen, it doesn't take thousands of words to start speaking with confidence. These 90+ phrases are small but mighty. They allow you to say hello, express thanks, ask questions, make new friends, and even face challenges—all with authenticity and warmth.

If all you did was master these phrases, you'd already be conversational. So take your time, revisit your favorites, and speak from the heart. And remember: Every phrase you say is one more step toward fluency.

Use them. Live them. Let them carry you into the next conversation.

Japanese	*Romaji*	English
こんにちは	*Konnichiwa*	Hello / Good afternoon
おはよう	*Ohayou*	Good morning
おやすみ	*Oyasumi*	Good night
ありがとう	*Arigatou*	Thank you
ありがとうございます	*Arigatou gozaimasu*	Thank you very much
すみません	*Sumimasen*	Excuse me / I'm sorry
ごめんなさい	*Gomennasai*	I'm sorry
はい	*Hai*	Yes
いいえ	*Iie*	No
どうぞ	*Douzo*	Here you go / Please
どうも	*Doumo*	Thanks / Hello
はじめまして	*Hajimemashite*	Nice to meet you
よろしくお願いします	*Yoroshiku onegaishimasu*	Please treat me well
お元気ですか?	*Ogenki desu ka?*	How are you?
元気です	*Genki desu*	I'm well

名前は何ですか？	*Namae wa nan desu ka?*	What's your name?
私の名前は〜です	*Watashi no namae wa ~ desu*	My name is ~
これは何ですか？	*Kore wa nan desu ka?*	What's this?
それは〜です	*Sore wa ~ desu*	That's ~
どこですか？	*Doko desu ka?*	Where is it?
トイレはどこですか？	*Toire wa doko desu ka?*	Where's the bathroom?
駅はどこ？	*Eki wa doko?*	Where's the station?
いくらですか？	*Ikura desu ka?*	How much is it?
これ、ください	*Kore, kudasai*	This, please
お願いします	*Onegaishimasu*	Please (formal)
メニューをください	*Menyuu o kudasai*	Menu, please
水をください	*Mizu o kudasai*	Water, please
おいしい！	*Oishii!*	Delicious!
まずい！	*Mazui!*	Tastes bad
たのしい！	*Tanoshii!*	Fun!
つまらない	*Tsumaranai*	Boring

かわいい!	*Kawaii!*	Cute!
かっこいい!	*Kakkoii!*	Cool!
すごい!	*Sugoi!*	Amazing!
いいね!	*Ii ne!*	Sounds good!
だめ	*Dame*	Not good / No way
大丈夫?	*Daijoubu?*	Are you okay?
大丈夫です	*Daijoubu desu*	I'm okay
気をつけて	*Ki wo tsukete*	Take care
行ってきます	*Ittekimasu*	I'm off (leaving home)
行ってらっしゃい	*Itterasshai*	See you later (response)
ただいま	*Tadaima*	I'm home
おかえり	*Okaeri*	Welcome back
いただきます	*Itadakimasu*	Let's eat (before meal)
ごちそうさまでした	*Gochisousama deshita*	Thank you for the meal
はやい!	*Hayai!*	Fast!
おそい	*Osoi*	Slow / Late
うれしい	*Ureshii*	Happy

かなしい	*Kanashii*	Sad
つかれた	*Tsukareta*	I'm tired
おなかすいた	*Onaka suita*	I'm hungry
ねむい	*Nemui*	Sleepy
わかりません	*Wakarimasen*	I don't understand
わかりました	*Wakarimashita*	I understood
もういちど	*Mou ichido*	One more time
ゆっくりお願いします	*Yukkuri onegaishimasu*	Slowly, please
英語で?	*Eigo de?*	In English?
何?	*Nani?*	What?
なぜ? / どうして?	*Naze? / Doushite?*	Why?
やった!	*Yatta!*	I did it! / Yay!
がんばれ!	*Ganbare!*	Do your best!
しんけんだ!	*Shinken da!*	I'm serious!
まけない!	*Makenai!*	I won't lose!
絶対に!	*Zettai ni!*	Absolutely!
さようなら	*Sayounara*	Goodbye
またね	*Mata ne*	See you again

じゃあね	*Jaa ne*	Later!
バイバイ	*Baibai*	Bye-bye
おめでとう!	*Omedetou!*	Congratulations!
誕生日おめでとう	*Tanjoubi omedetou*	Happy birthday!
お久しぶりです	*Ohisashiburi desu*	Long time no see
初めてです	*Hajimete desu*	It's my first time
楽しみにしてます	*Tanoshimi ni shitemasu*	I'm looking forward to it
気にしないで	*Ki ni shinaide*	Don't worry about it
本当?	*Hontou?*	Really?
うそ!	*Uso!*	No way! / You're kidding!
手伝ってくれてありがとう	*Tetsudatte kurete arigatou*	Thanks for your help
感謝します	*Kansha shimasu*	I'm truly grateful
お疲れ様です	*Otsukaresama desu*	Thank you for your hard work
よくできました	*Yoku dekimashita*	Well done
すみません、わかりません	*Sumimasen, wakarimasen*	Sorry, I don't understand
道に迷いました	*Michi ni mayoimashita*	I'm lost

助けて!	*Tasukete!*	Help!
警察!	*Keisatsu!*	Police!
病院はどこ?	*Byouin wa doko?*	Where's the hospital?
気持ち悪いです	*Kimochi warui desu*	I feel sick
少しだけ話せます	*Sukoshi dake hanasemasu*	I can speak a little
日本語を勉強しています	*Nihongo o benkyou shiteimasu*	I'm studying Japanese
日本が大好きです	*Nihon ga daisuki desu*	I love Japan
趣味は何ですか?	*Shumi wa nan desu ka?*	What's your hobby?
趣味はアニメです	*Shumi wa anime desu*	My hobby is anime
漫画が好きです	*Manga ga suki desu*	I like manga
ゲームしますか?	*Geemu shimasu ka?*	Do you play games?
いいえ、しません	*Iie, shimasen*	No, I don't
はい、します!	*Hai, shimasu!*	Yes, I do!

40+ Essential Kanji

Kanji may look intimidating at first, but each character is a tiny story, a piece of history, a visual symbol, and a key to unlocking Japanese meaning and culture. The 40+ kanji in this section were handpicked to give you a powerful foundation. These are the kanji you'll actually see and use in daily life.

From counting to traveling, eating to expressing emotions, these characters appear on signs, menus, websites, manga pages, and more. As you learn them, you'll begin to recognize patterns, build reading fluency, and feel a sense of familiarity in a language that once looked like a sea of symbols.

Kanji doesn't have to be overwhelming. With a little context and curiosity, it becomes exciting.

Now that you've seen these 40+ essential kanji, you've taken a huge leap toward real literacy. You're no longer staring at characters in confusion; you're recognizing meaning, making connections, and engaging with Japanese on a deeper level.

Each kanji you've learned is a symbol of your growth. Keep reviewing them in context. Notice them in signs, anime, and daily interactions. Let them become friends you recognize.

You don't have to learn all 2,000 in one night. You've already started with the most important ones. And that's how fluency begins: one meaningful character at a time.

Kanji	*Romaji*	English
人	*Hito*	Person
手	*Te*	Hand
一	*Ichi*	One
二	*Ni*	Two
三	*San*	Three
四	*Shi / Yon*	Four
五	*Go*	Five
六	*Roku*	Six
七	*Shichi / Nana*	Seven
八	*Hachi*	Eight
九	*Kyuu*	Nine
十	*Juu*	Ten
円	*En*	Yen / Circle
日	*Hi / Nichi*	Day / Sun
月	*Tsuki / Getsu*	Month / Moon
火	*Hi / Ka*	Fire
水	*Mizu / Sui*	Water
木	*Ki / Moku*	Tree / Wood

金	*Kane / Kin*	Gold / Money
土	*Tsuchi / Do*	Earth
本	*Hon*	Book / Origin
学	*Gaku*	Study
校	*Kou*	School
名	*Na / Mei*	Name
食	*Shoku / Tabe*	Eat
飲	*In / No*	Drink
行	*I / Kou*	Go
来	*Rai / Ku*	Come
見	*Mi / Ken*	See
話	*Hanashi / Wa*	Talk / Speak
聞	*Ki / Bun*	Hear
書	*Sho / Kaku*	Write
読	*Doku / Yomu*	Read
車	*Kuruma / Sha*	Car
駅	*Eki*	Station
時	*Toki / Ji*	Time / Hour
何	*Nani / Nan*	What

感	*Kan*	Feeling
謝	*Sha / Ayama*	Apology
愛	*Ai*	Love
力	*Chikara*	Strength

Final Encouragement

Read this when you feel behind. Or tired. Or unsure.

Let's take a deep breath together.

You don't need to do everything at once. You don't need to master every kanji by next month. You don't need to have perfect pronunciation. You don't need to catch up to someone else's progress.

Your journey isn't late. It's not broken. It's yours.

And here's what you do need:

1. A Plan That Fits Your Life

Not someone else's 3-hour-a-day cram routine. Just your pace. Your windows of time. Your rhythm. Even if it's 10 minutes in the morning and 5 minutes at night. That counts.

2. Curiosity About the Language and the Culture

Not just about passing a test, but about wanting to understand the world through new words, new ways of seeing, and small "aha" moments. Like noticing how いただきます isn't just "Let's eat," but a whisper of gratitude. Or how the same word can change tone and meaning depending on the speaker's heart.

3. The Courage to Keep Showing Up—Even When It's Messy

Even when you forget how to say something simple. Even when you accidentally call someone's dog "delicious" instead of "cute." Even when your voice shakes or your mind blanks. That's not failure. That's real learning.

And guess what?

You already have all of that. If you made it this far—through the pages, the practice, the pauses—you've already proven that you're serious, curious, and brave.

Keep showing up. Keep saying what you can. Keep learning your way.

You've got this. And 日本語 (*ni-hon-go*) is lucky to have you.

またね。(See you again.)

END

Made in United States
Troutdale, OR
01/18/2026

45658573R00120